GCSE

English Exam Techniques

a 12-week revision programme

Keith Brindle

Introduction

Your questions answered.

Q: What is the point of this book?
A: The aims of this book are:

- to give a **clear insight** into the skills you need to succeed in GCSE English exams
- to show **when** and **where** those skills need to be demonstrated
- to **practise** those skills, and give the opportunity to **develop** them **on your own**
- to **explain** how your **work is marked** by examiners
- to **provide** a **structured programme** that leads right up to the exams themselves

and most important of all,

- to **enable you to gain those extra marks** which will improve your chance of **a higher grade**.

Q: But you can't revise English, can you?
A: English may not appear to be a subject with lots of facts, figures or formulae, but, like any other subject, it has component parts and skills that can be practised and learned. This book has a series of structured units which will focus on those parts and skills.

Q: How can this book help me get a better grade, then?
A: You should work through the book, unit by unit. However, if this is not possible, you can focus on key pages or sections which you – or your teacher – consider problematic. As you will see, the book has a clear structure which is easy to follow.

Q: So, how is this book structured?
A: There are 12 units (plus a final checklist) – which could fit the 12 weeks before your exam. Each one deals with a key aspect of the English exam, whether it's *'Knowing the Papers'* or *'Writing to Argue, Persuade, Advise'*. The units vary in length, but offer you:

- an opening section which gives **advice** and **information**
- **practice**, often in 'bite-sized' tasks
- **further practice**, with more developed writing
- the knowledge of how to **move up a grade**, using the key skills the examiners are hoping to find in your work.

Q: Is there anything else to help me?
A: Yes. On many pages the author of the book, a senior examiner offers **Examiner's Tips** – that is, key pointers to improve your work. Also, each unit ends with a **summary** of the main points covered.

Q: Sounds great. When can I get started?
A: Any time you like! Just turn the page.

Keith Brindle

Contents

Unit 1 Knowing the Papers

Targets

1. **To understand the different parts of the examination.**
2. **To know what is tested in English Paper 1.**
3. **To know what is tested in English Paper 2.**

General Information

Many candidates in the country are entered for this examination: AQA, Specification B. So, to be successful you need to be well prepared. This book will help you stay ahead of the competition.

details

English GCSE

Coursework:	**40% of final mark**	**20% for written coursework (Reading and Writing)** **20% for Speaking and Listening**
Examinations:	**60% of final mark**	**30% for Paper 1** **30% for Paper 2**

Paper 1 lasts 1 hour 40 minutes
Paper 2 lasts 1 hour 30 minutes

The English Literature examination, for which you might also be entered, has coursework and one paper lasting 2 hours 15 minutes. English Literature is a separate subject and candidates are awarded a separate grade.

In this book, we will be dealing exclusively with the English examinations.

What you need for your English examinations

Pens, pencils, a ruler.
For 2004, your copy of the pre-released material; for 2005 and beyond, a new copy will be provided in the examination itself.

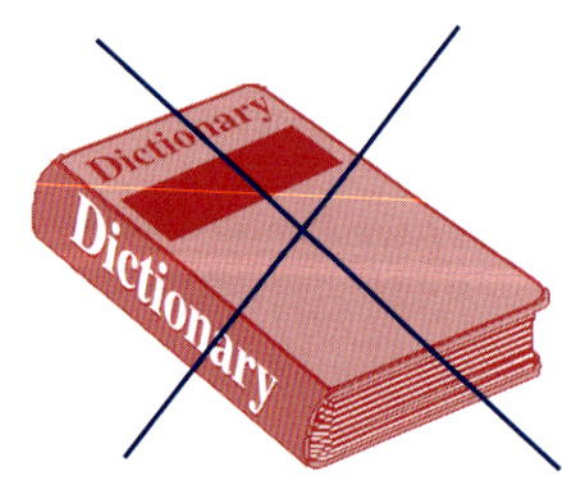

Dictionaries are not allowed.

However, when you turn up on the 'big day' you also need to be properly prepared. You need to know:

- what is being tested
- what the examiner wants to see
- and how to produce excellent answers.

If you arrive in the examination room knowing what is expected of you, you can approach the papers confidently.

English Paper 1

- Lasts 1 hour 40 minutes.
- Contains two sections:
  Section A, dealing with media and non-fiction texts, should take an hour.
  Section B, writing to argue, persuade, advise, should take 40 minutes.

FACTS

- Time
- Tasks

Stick to the time that's advised – it's the time the task should take.

EXAMINER'S TIP!

Section A

Media texts

These will be printed in the pre-released booklet, given to candidates in January so that they can be studied in advance. They will be chosen from a range of materials, written for different purposes and audiences: articles, advertisements, cartoons, reports, web pages and so on. You will probably be asked to compare two of these texts.

Non-fiction text

The paper will also contain a previously unseen non-fiction text, which you will read and then write about.

Section B

There will be just one question, requiring you to argue, persuade or advise or to produce a response involving two or three of these skills.

English Paper 2

- Lasts 1 hour 30 minutes
- Contains two sections:
  Section A, dealing with poetry from different cultures and traditions, should take 45 minutes.
  Section B, writing to analyse, review, comment, should also take 45 minutes.

FACTS

- Time
- Tasks

Section A

Poetry from Different Cultures and Traditions

The pre-released booklet will contain eight to ten poems written by poets from different cultures around the world. The poems will be studied before the examination. You have to answer **one question**, comparing one of the poems with a poem you have not seen before, printed on the examination paper.

Section B

There will be just one question, asking you to analyse, review or comment or to write using two or three of these skills.

The Assessment of Reading

Your reading is being tested in Section A of each examination. The two papers test your ability to:

- *analyse texts, refer to them and say what they mean*
- *write about facts and opinions, how they are used and how information is presented*
- *follow and analyse an argument*
- *compare texts*
- *explain how writers use language, structural devices and presentational devices.*

All these skills could be tested on Paper 1, Section A.

The poetry question on Paper 2 is most likely to focus on analysis of meaning, language and structure and on comparison. It will also test your ability to understand the culture about which the poem is written, or the culture from which the poet has come.

The Assessment of Writing

The mark schemes for both Section B questions expect examiners to consider:

- *content: the ideas and information you include*
- *your ability to write for a given purpose and audience*
- *your ability to organise your writing, so that what is said flows effectively and logically*
- *language*
- *paragraphing*
- *sentences*
- *spelling and handwriting.*

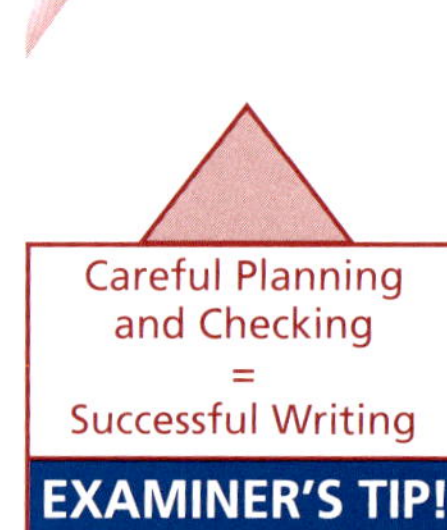

Successful writing requires careful planning and checking. To improve your marks, take time to structure your ideas and save five minutes at the end to correct your mistakes.

In both examinations your priorities should be clear:

1. Answer the questions that have been set.
2. In Section A of both papers (the reading section):
   - focus on how effects have been achieved, rather than just what is being said
   - make clear comparisons when they are required
   - language and how it is used will be the most important element in most answers.
3. In Section B of both papers (the writing section):
   - planning is likely to improve your marks
   - responses should be suited to purpose and audience
   - checking to improve the writing is vital.

Re-read this unit, then answer the following questions:

Knowing the Papers

How much have you remembered?

1. Which examination paper involves the pre-released poetry?
2. How many poems from different cultures and traditions will you probably have to write about?
3. How long should you spend on Paper 2, Section A?
4. What kind of essay will you write in Section B of Paper 1?
5. In Paper 1, how long should you spend on Section A?
6. How long do you have to answer Paper 1?
7. How long do you have to answer Paper 2?
8. What kind of essay will you write in Section B of Paper 2?
9. What reading skills will be tested?
10. How many questions, in total, will you answer on each paper?

Unit 2 Reading Media Texts

To focus on:

1. **Purpose and audience.**
2. **How presentation and language are used.**
3. **The skills that will be tested in the examination.**

The media texts you study will be in the pre-released booklet. There will be six to ten texts, from a variety of sources. For example:

- advertisements
- newspaper articles
- cartoons
- reports
- web pages
- newspaper editorials or leaders and so on.

Exam Preparation

Read Widely **Read Regularly**

The more media texts you read, the better you will understand how they work: what they are aiming to do, how they are trying to achieve their aims and what audience they are targeting.

When you read a media text, you should recognise its:

- **purpose** – why the text was produced
- **audience** – the people for whom it was written.

The text's effect will be gained by:

- **presentational devices** and **layout**
- **language**.

Its success depends on how well it:

- **fulfils its purpose**
- **appeals** to its **target audience**.

Task 1

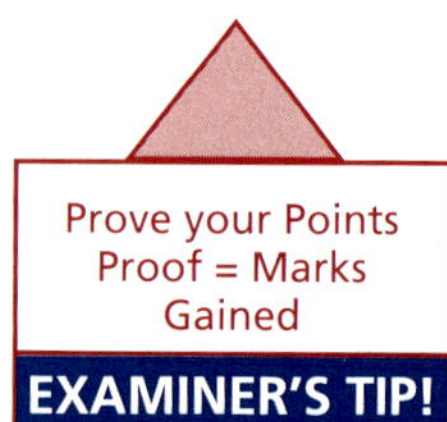

Consider the example opposite and decide:

- **what exactly is the purpose and target audience for this product**
- **how it is attempting to appeal to its audience through presentational devices and language**
- **how successful it is likely to be. Give reasons.**

GET BLITZED!

TODAY!

BLITZED ISN'T THE SORT OF CHOCOLATE BAR
YOU'D GIVE TO YOUR GRANNY…

This is how two students responded to the question:

Response 1
The advert is for a chocolate bar you wouldn't give your granny. They are trying to get you to buy it. It's called 'Blitzed' and on the advert there is a picture of a boy who looks weird. People like that will probably buy it …

Response 2
Any advertisement tries to get you to buy a product, and this one is no different. The chocolate bar is new and is clearly aimed at young people. The picture is to make you think people who buy the bar are different from the older generation – free to be what they want to be; and even the name of the bar will attract the target audience, because 'Blitzed' sounds like some kind of new drug …

Task 2

1. **Which response is better? Why?**
2. **What else might have been added to Response 2?**
3. **How good is your response, in comparison?**

When analysing layout and presentation, always try to:

- Bear in mind the target audience.
- Examine the particular effect of a picture:
  - Does it make us sympathetic/angry/suspicious/laugh/better informed? Why/how?
  - Would a different picture create a different impact?
- Decide why particular colours have been used:
  - red might indicate anger or violence, love or danger or …
  - blue might seem very conservative or restful or …
  - green might seem peaceful or environmentally friendly or …
- Judge the possible effects of text boxes, headings, sub-headings, designs, particular fonts and their size and so on.

When analysing the language used, always try to:

- Bear in mind the target audience.
- Say why particular words or phrases have been used, rather than just listing devices.
- Use the sort of techniques employed when studying literature: select linguistic features and say what effect each one has, or is intended to have. (For example: *When 'TODAY!' is used as a one-word sentence, it is as if someone is shouting at the reader.*)

If you use the correct vocabulary to comment on texts, your responses will be much more precise.

Task 3

Make sure you know the meaning of all the following terms:

Language/style:

Standard English, conversational, formal, informal, argumentative, persuasive, factual, opinionated, informative, patronising, journalistic, slang, subjective, objective, facts, opinions, figures, metaphors, similes, alliteration, onomatopoeia, emotive, rhetorical, repetition, quotation, irony.

Presentation/layout:

bullet points, columns, headings, sub-headings, illustrations, diagrams, italics, bold print, font, justified, centred, logos, icons, symbols, headlines, margin, byline, indent, photographs, prose, verse, image, foreground, background, shot, frame, angle, connotation.

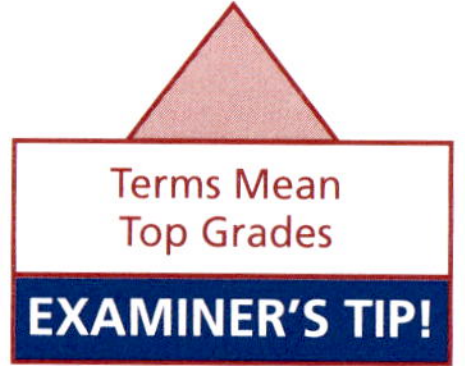

Technical terms are worth revising. Used appropriately, they impress the examiner.

Television standards topple

'No nourishment for couch potatoes,' says report.

The latest review of television standards makes depressing reading. According to Teleview, the independent viewing commission, we are subjected to more repeats and more 'dumbing down' of programmes than ever before. Rather than liberating our viewing habits, digital TV is giving us only programmes we have seen before, cheap-to-make 'rubbish' and cartoons for the kids. Our minds are not stimulated but we still do not turn off …

Task 4

1. **What is the purpose and the audience for this text? Explain your views.**
2. **How is language used by the writer?**

Purpose
To entertain? To inform? To persuade? To mock?

Audience
Children? Parents? Teachers?

Remember:
Make quotations clear by using inverted commas, and indent longer quotations:

The writer tries to amuse the reader by linking 'nourishment' and 'potatoes':
'No nourishment for couch potatoes.'
He wants us to think that …

The technique, which should be practised, is –

- make a point
- prove it
- explain it.

3. **How might presentational devices have been used to make the article more striking?**

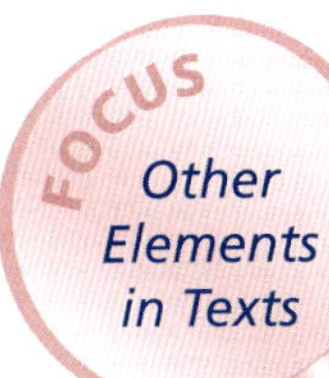

Some media texts you study will allow the examiner to set questions on more than just presentation and language, of course. There are other elements tested in the media texts section. For example:

- how **facts and opinions** are used
- how **arguments** are put together
- how texts are **structured**.

Facts: can be proven, give the reader confidence in the writer, make texts seem believable, highlight particular details.

Opinions: are what someone thinks, may not be true, try to convince a reader, intend to persuade, can appear logical.

Arguments: usually have an introduction and conclusion, use a range of techniques such as contrasts, examples, quotations, facts and opinions, emotive language, irony, humour, discourse markers to link ideas, exaggeration, anecdotes and are intended to lead us to accept a point of view.

Structures: can vary: sometimes the text is balanced, or begins with a general point and moves to be more precise, or begins with a precise example and then generalises, or begins with humour and ends with despair, or has clear and different sections.

Read the newspaper report below.

Students bored to breaking point

"I just said what everyone else was thinking," says student excluded for speaking out.

Is it time our outdated approaches to schooling came into line with the modern world? That is the question being debated in a small town in the Midlands after a fifteen-year-old pupil was excluded from school for saying he found assembly boring.

Elliott: "I'm no troublemaker."

Elliott Byron had never been in serious trouble throughout his life at Durnhill High School in Barton, Warwickshire, until he dared to write to the local paper, complaining about his headteacher's assemblies. Then he was suspended.

"I come to school to learn, not to be bored every morning," said Elliott. And, despite the fact that most children feel the same way about assembly, Mrs Garland, his headteacher, was not amused.

Elliott is unrepentant: "I'm only saying what others say. But the teachers are treating me like a bully or a vandal. I thought we had the right to speak out in this country. The other children say I'm a hero now, so I'm not going to say sorry. Why should I?"

PRACTICE

Task 5

1. **How are facts and opinions used?**
   You could begin:
   The facts tell us what has happened to Elliott. For example, he has been suspended from school. Also … . However, the opinions seem to present him in a positive light: he 'dared' to write a letter of complaint, so he sounds … ; and …

2. **How is the argument developed?**
   Consider:
   - **the headline**
   - **the first question ('Is it time … ')**
   - **how the question is answered**
   - **how Elliott is contrasted with Mrs Garland**
   - **who has the final word.**

3. **How is the article structured?**
   Consider:
   - **the opening quotation and the ending**
   - **the effect of how the second, third and fourth paragraphs begin**
   - **how the article focuses almost exclusively on Elliott's views.**

Task 6

Inventing any details or quotations you require, produce a newspaper article on Elliott's problems, which is more critical of him.

Remember to:
- keep purpose and audience in mind
- structure your argument effectively
- use appropriate presentation, layout and language
- include both facts and opinions.

Task 7

Analyse the effectiveness of your argument, presentation, language and use of facts and opinions.

This is a newspaper report:

Fake Lords Mock our Visitors

To get our own back on the Americans might appear praise-worthy – but is it? For years now they have looked down on their 'cute little old cousins' in Europe so it can be a delight to see a Texan look foolish. Especially if he wears a large Stetson hat and checked trousers, of course.

However, a scam to trick Americans and take their cash under false pretences has been discovered, and are the police laughing? Not at all.

J.C. Tucker, a Texan oil baron, has complained of being defrauded of over £2000 by Lord Wacket of Windlebury. He paid the cash to stay on his Lordship's country estate for a week, as one of 20 house guests. But he realised, during a £400-a-head banquet, that his host was not in fact Lord Wacket, but an actor, Timothy Dalford. He was playing the part of Wacket for the holiday season.

Timothy Dalford

The police sent in a top team. The enquiries have produced four arrests, and an extended investigation. A probe of other mansions in the surrounding counties has found that over 40% run scams along similar lines. Americans are the main targets. "They can afford it, though," said one admirer of Lord Wacket.

J.C. Tucker is in Cannes, recovering, and does not wish to comment.

Task 8

How successful is this report?
Comment on:

- **purpose and audience**
- **layout and presentational devices**
- **the language used**
- **the effect of the facts and opinions**
- **the structure of the report and the points it makes.**

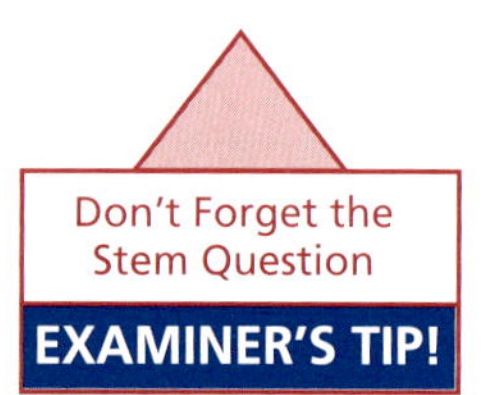

When responding to bullet points, don't forget the main, 'stem' question (in this case, 'How successful is this report?').

Here are three extracts from students' responses:

F Grade
The report is written for a newspaper. It says how Americans are good to laugh at. There's a picture of Timothy Dalford and a headline to make us read it. The language tells us about the cheating that was taking place and there are facts like the £2000 paid to Lord Wacket of Windlebury …

C Grade
This seems a successful report, probably from a broadsheet newspaper because the sentences are long and there are legal terms like 'defrauded'. The picture, though, attracts readers, because the title refers to 'Fake Lords' and Timothy Dalford does look like a rich person, but very fake, so we know that he's the one fooling visitors …

A Grade
The text is challenging, and probably written for a broadsheet newspaper. The style is appropriate. For instance, the picture of Timothy Dalford is like a formal portrait; though it looks like he's had plastic surgery, so he looks untrustworthy, like a 'Fake Lord'. However, the opening is a rhetorical question, which asks us first to consider our attitude to Americans. It offers the opinion that Americans patronise us ('cute little old cousins'), but they are presented as figures of fun, with 'Stetsons' and clown-like 'checked trousers' …

Task 9

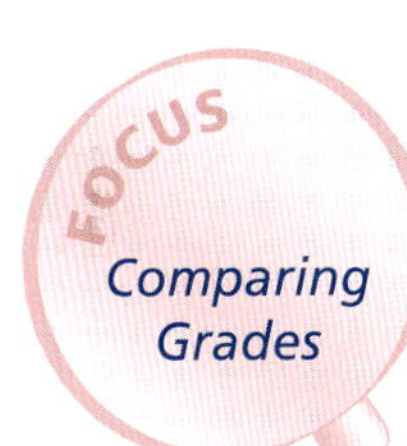

1. **Look at the 'F Grade' response. Is the candidate explaining how successful the report seems? Is there any analysis of the text?**
2. **Why is the 'C Grade' response better?**
3. **Say why the final extract is best. Examine how the student:**
   - **deals with the stem of the question as well as the bullets**
   - **selects and uses appropriate material**
   - **employs an effective vocabulary.**

Task 10

Continue the 'A Grade' response, using the skills you have just identified.

- Read widely, to develop your understanding and skills, and practise on other texts.
- Prepare to write about purpose and audience, presentational devices, argument, facts and opinions, language and structure.
- Learn and use an appropriate vocabulary.

Unit 3 Responding to Media Texts in the Examination

Targets

1. **To understand and answer the sorts of questions that will be in the media text section of Paper 1.**
2. **To focus on what is tested and how to respond.**
3. **To examine different types of questions, for Specification B and for Specification B (Mature).**

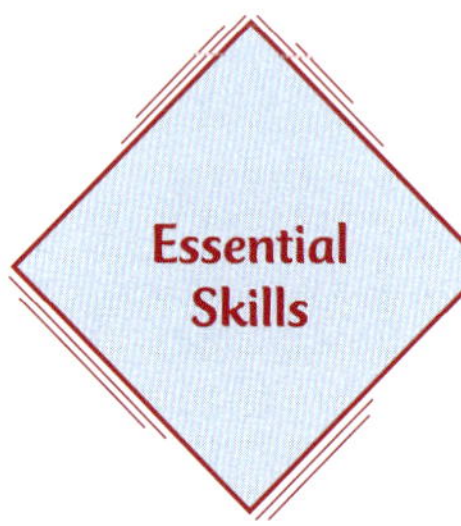

Section A of Paper 1 is designed to take an hour.
There are two questions:

- Question 1: on two or more media texts (30 minutes)
- Question 2: on a previously unseen non-fiction extract (30 minutes).

This unit will help you cope with Question 1.

How to produce your answer

1. Read the question carefully, underlining the important words.
2. Re-read the texts that you will be addressing in your answer, underlining those details you intend to include in your answer.
3. Write your answer, ensuring that you respond to the question and each bullet point and quote appropriately.

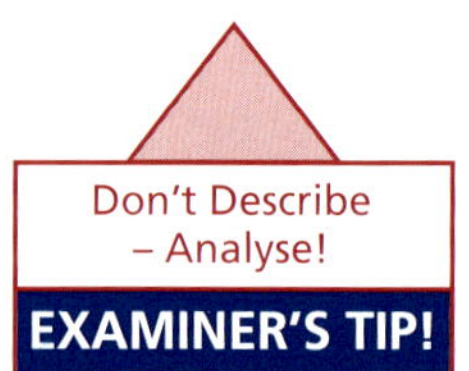

When answering questions, try to analyse rather than describe. To gain higher marks, say what effect is created by elements of a text, rather than just describing them.

There is a picture of a man in a bath and a rubber duck and a towel is on the floor and …

Heading for Grade G

The illustration highlights the main message: that some men never grow up. The duck represents …

Heading for Grade A*

Types of question

The examiners might set different types of questions, but two kinds are most likely, depending on which specification you sit:

Specification B (Main Paper)

There may well be a general question, followed by a series of bullets requiring close focus on particular texts. For example:

How do the different texts try to interest the reader in their subject?

Explain:
- *how the cartoons are presented*
- *the way in which the main viewpoint is structured in the article 'The old are no longer loved'*
- *how the writer tries to convince us that he is right in the leader column headed 'Cuts in services inevitable'.*

Which skills are being tested here?

1. Overall, the ability to select appropriate material.
2. Stem question: ability to analyse texts.
3. Bullet 1: ability to evaluate of structural and presentational devices.
4. Bullet 2: ability to follow an argument and identify structure.
5. Bullet 3: ability to follow an argument – and possibly to evaluate linguistic devices and the use of facts and opinions.

Task 1

Identify the important words in the question, as you would in the examination.

By focusing on the important words, you avoid the temptation to include information and analysis that is not required. With only 30 minutes at your disposal, you must call upon the knowledge you have gained by studying the pre-released texts before the examination, but you will not have to write 'everything you know'.

When you have decided what a question is requiring you to do, you have to find the necessary points in your media texts.

Read these texts:

The Fur's still flying:

'Cockatrice' released this week

Incredibly, after 20 years as an 'underground' band, Foxfur are still being courted by the top record labels. And, on this latest showing from the hottest rock property never to have a hit single, they look set to continue for many years more.

For their latest CD, 'Cockatrice', they have produced 12 tracks which move from the sultry R & B strains of Van Morrison in his prime to echoes of Ozzy Osbourne and then the control of Toploader. Yet it never turns into some kind of sad and varied sampler: the lead vocals of Jimmy Forrest never weaken, and the distinctive harmonies of Jenny and Sue Lin tie the tracks together.

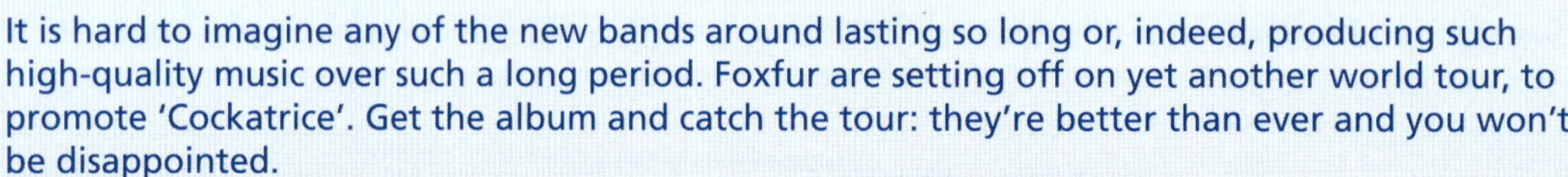

It is hard to imagine any of the new bands around lasting so long or, indeed, producing such high-quality music over such a long period. Foxfur are setting off on yet another world tour, to promote 'Cockatrice'. Get the album and catch the tour: they're better than ever and you won't be disappointed.

Reviewed by Janie Robinson

Internews Online

Politics | International Affairs | Government

Latest Stocks and Shares | European Union | Parliament Now

- Showbiz
- Weather
- Television
- Media World
- Sports Update

Search

Recession Deepens

Chancellor's latest predictions

Music industry meltdown?

Shares in the music industry plummeted today, as top record company EMG Corporate announced huge losses.

At a time when share prices are falling, house prices still rising and wage increases are so low, the music industry was bound to suffer eventually. EMG have recently cancelled tours by top artists Gareth Yates and DJ Giles following poor ticket sales. Now they intend to reduce the number of their new releases. They are also cutting acts from their lists in an attempt to weather the financial storm. They say they have no alternative.

CD sales fell by an astonishing 34% in the last six months. "This sort of situation spells disaster," said Chief Executive Piers Manson at the EMG press conference this morning. "Whether it can be blamed in part on the fact that people simply have little spare money to spend, I don't know. What is certain is that with so many young people downloading tracks free from the net and with so few artists producing original material, the world of pop music is in crisis. As a company, we have to cut our losses immediately, or we will not stay afloat."

Task 2

What impression of the pop music industry is presented in these two texts? Respond to each of the following prompts.

- **Comment on the presentational devices in the article 'The Fur's still flying'.**
- **How does the language in 'The Fur's still flying' appeal to its target audience?**
- **In 'Music industry meltdown?', what is the justification for the changes EMG are making?**
- **How does EMG use facts to support its case?**

Remember:
You are supposed to be considering the impression of the music industry that is being presented whilst you discuss what is required by the bullet points.

Consider:

Under Bullet 1: the effect of the picture, whether the layout (headline, sub-heading, paragraphing) creates any particular impression

Under Bullet 2: the use of significant words, for example: *'incredibly'*, *'And … '*, *'hottest rock property'*, *'latest CD'*, *'sultry … strains'*, *'get'*, *'catch'* and so on

Under Bullet 3: the way the argument is built by the writer and by Piers Manson

Under Bullet 4: balancing the use of facts, such as *'sales fell by 34%'*, against the use of opinions like *'This sort of situation spells disaster'*.

Specification B (Mature): For Post-16 Centres

On the Mature paper, there will probably be a comparative question on two texts, followed by bullets clarifying which elements should be compared. For example:

Compare the Oxfam web page and the report from Steven McCirrick in Bangladesh. Write about:

- *who they blame for the conditions*
- *how they justify their opinions*
- *the language they use to convince their readers*
- *which text is most successful.*

Which skills are being tested here?

1. Overall ability to select appropriate material.
2. Stem question: ability to compare texts.
3. Bullet 1: ability to follow an argument.
4. Bullet 2: ability to follow an argument, and possibly to analyse structure and the uses of fact and opinion.
5. Bullet 3: ability to evaluate the use of language.
6. Bullet 4: ability to evaluate the effectiveness of elements in texts.

Task 3

In an examination, which words in the question would you underline?

An important element in this style of question is that the comparative element runs through each bullet point. Therefore, candidates in the examination are likely to structure their response logically – for example:

- **a.** blame in web page
- **b.** blame in report
- **c.** how the opinion is justified in the web page
- **d.** how the opinion is justified in the report.

However, it is important to link ideas clearly, using a **comparative vocabulary**. For example: *on the other hand, similarly, in the same way, in contrast, whereas, just as … so … , however, in comparison, but* and so on.

Look at this example of a comparative approach:

> *'Whereas the web page implies that funding should be found by national governments, John McCirrick takes a different approach …'*

Read the following texts:

Offenders reformed by victims

New method proves effective in changing criminals' lives

The Home Office recently released details of an experiment which has brought together young offenders and their victims. The face-to-face meetings have been producing remarkable results.

Statistics show that most young offenders reoffend within two years. Incredibly, the figure can be as high as 89% for 15- and 16-year-olds. This is a situation which has been allowed to continue for years because there has been no system put in place, to change the ways of criminals. Imprisonment punishes them, but does not make them reform their ways.

However, Leeds Probation Service has been trialling a new approach. Victim and offender sit down together, and the victim learns why the offender committed the crime.

More importantly, the offender has to take responsibility for what he or she has done. Put simply: the offenders, when they have to listen to the sufferings of the victims, realise the errors of their ways. They get to know the real person they have hurt. The aptly named PC Dove says: "You can turn someone's life around. Often, these are not bad young people; they simply did a bad thing."

PC Dove and those who work with him seem to have a point: 68% of youngsters involved in the project have not reoffended after two years. One boy summed up what has happened to him: "My life's changed 'cos I made it change." And that seems to sum up the success of the venture.

Task 4

How might the reader react to the kind of people prisoners seem to be in these texts?
Compare them, by writing about:

- **the language used**
- **visual impact**
- **their purpose and audience.**

Advice:

Deal with one bullet at a time.

Use comparing words.

Examiner's Summary

- Identify the key words and deal with the precise requirements of the question.
- Bear in mind both the stem question and the bullets.
- If making comparisons, use appropriate comparative vocabulary.

Unit 4 Reading Non-fiction Texts

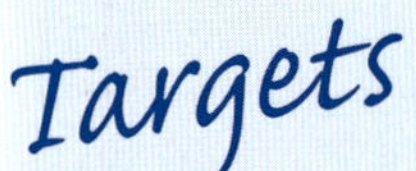

To focus on:

1. **what will be tested in the examination**
2. **the kind of questions that will be asked**
3. **how to respond to the questions.**

Having spent 30 minutes responding to questions about the media texts on Paper 1, Section A, you will then have 30 minutes to write about a non-fiction text. It will be printed on the examination paper and you will not have seen it in advance.

You will have to:

- find out what the unseen text is about
- read the question
- read the text carefully, bearing in mind the question
- locate the information and ideas required to answer the question
- write your answer.

Questions

As with the media question, you will have to interpret the text and might be required to write about:

- ideas
- facts and opinions
- argument
- structure
- language
- why the text is successful.

Your priorities should be to provide the information and evaluation required and to prove your points by referring to the text.

Consider this extract from a biographical article about actress, Renee Zellweger:

> But Zellweger has more than her physical assets to offer. She's a versatile actress with a natural comic ability. She can look sensational, as seen at the Oscars, and also wonderfully natural, as now, in jeans and a cashmere top, sipping her favourite soya milk latte in a Hollywood café. She's also friendly, chatty and polite. And she never takes her fame for granted. "You walk down a red carpet and people scream your name and clap, for what? Because you're lucky. It's not talent," she explains.
>
> Modesty in the face of multi-million-dollar pay cheques and movie star boyfriends must be difficult. But her self-deprecating vulnerability is genuine. How else could a leading actress be in the ladies' room when Hugh Grant is waiting on stage to present her with a Golden Globe? "I was wiping lipstick off my teeth," she giggles, referring to the Best Actress in Musical or Comedy award she won last year for her role in *Nurse Betty*.
>
> by Elaine Lipworth in *Sky Customer Magazine*

Task 1

How does the writer argue that Renee Zellweger deserves our approval? Complete these tables.

Facts and opinions		Impression created of Zellweger
Facts	1. attended Oscars 2. drinks soya milk latte 3. 4.	
Opinions	1. versatile actress with natural comic ability 2. can look sensational 3. 4.	

Structure of extract		Impression created of Zellweger
First paragraph	1. begins by suggesting various sides to the actress 2. 3.	
Second paragraph	1. moves on to her modesty 2. 3.	

Emotive language		Impression created of Zellweger
1. sensational 2. friendly 3.	4. 5. 6.	

The Charge of the Light Brigade is famous in British history. In the Crimean War, the pride of the cavalry were sent down a valley from which there was no escape. They were massacred by Russians on the hills above. This is how they returned:

> The pace was heartbreakingly slow; most survivors were on foot; little groups of men dragged along, step by step, leaning on each other … The wreckage of men and horses was piteous. 'What a scene of havoc was this last mile – strewn with the dead and dying and all friends!' wrote Lord George Paget … Painfully, step by step, under heavy fire, the exhausted, bleeding remnants of the Light Brigade dragged themselves back to safety … Men ran down to meet their comrades and wrung them by the hand, as if they had struggled back from the depths of hell itself …
>
> Some 700 horsemen had charged down the valley, and 195 had returned. The 17th Lancers was reduced to thirty-seven troopers, the 13th Light Dragoons could muster only two officers and eight mounted men; 500 horses had been killed.
>
> *The Reason Why* by Cecil Woodham-Smith

Question

What impression of the event is created in this extract?
In your answer, discuss:

- the use of fact and opinion
- language.

Answer

Facts and opinions are used to let us know what it was like. One fact is '500 horses had been killed.' Another is: 'most survivors were on foot.' There is an opinion too: 'heartbreakingly slow'. The language makes it all real, like 'exhausted' and 'charged down the valley'.

Task 2

How good is this answer?

Decide:

- how it could have been improved
- what should have been added.

These are extracts from a better answer:

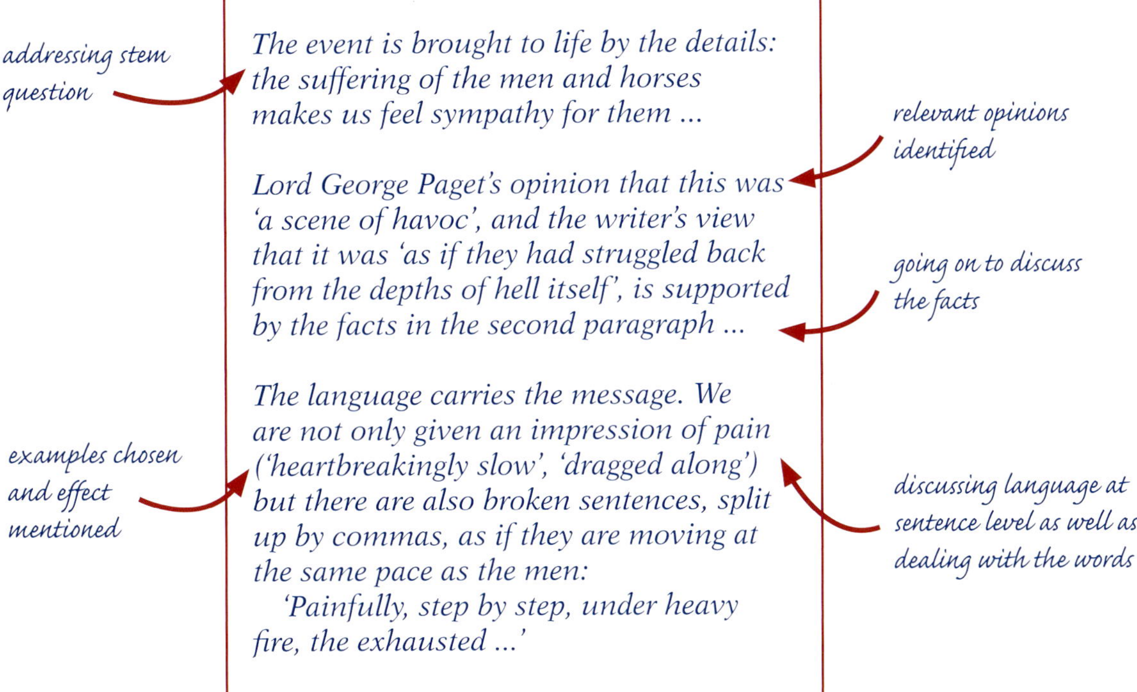

Task 3

The answer above is only an extract. Develop it, to include all the possible relevant points, focusing on:

- **the overall impression**
- **facts, opinions and how they are used**
- **particular uses of language.**

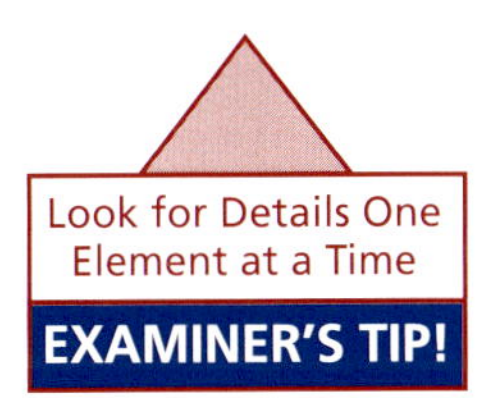

Work through the extract, looking for the details required for each element of the question in turn. Explain the effects created and quote appropriately.

In the examination, you will have to deal with a much longer text, like this one.

Your Holiday Disaster

At last they found somewhere in Turkey that had not been invaded by British tourists. But if the locals seemed pleased to see them, there was a cat who, evidently, was not.
By *Keith Brindle*

On our first evening in Turkey, we ate lamb and savouries and drank wine and raki. There were very few British tourists in Datca. We dined in a restaurant, halfway up the bustling, aromatic main street. When someone told a joke, my wife, Samantha, exploded with laughter. Unfortunately, there was a cat beside her chair, next to her trailing arm. As she raised her hands to cover her mouth, the cat was startled and bit her, badly.

Next morning, her hand was swollen. The local doctor pulled it around. Samantha cried. He sent us to the hospital, where no one spoke English or French or German. We felt very foreign and Samantha was terrified. We were taken into a consulting room, which was full of flies. Used syringes lay around; there was blood on the walls. Another doctor pulled and pressed Samantha's hand again, whilst speaking in Turkish to the nurse.

The only word I recognised was 'rubies'. "You mean rabies?" I asked, when he had finished. He shrugged: "Rabies. Yes. Possible." He talked with me and ignored Samantha. He explained, somehow, that she must have five injections, one every two days. I shuddered. With no real hope, I pointed at my arm. "Here?" "No," he said, pointing to his own stomach, "umbilical."

Outside, I explained to Samantha that we must go to the chemist for syringes; that she could have rabies; that she must have injections in her stomach. She was devastated. I had seen a television programme about the treatment and I was the one who bent over to be sick.

We returned to the consulting room because we had to. Samantha lay down. A male orderly stroked her hair. A nurse poked at her tummy button before plunging in the syringe. Apparently, the needle entering the stomach is painful, but the serum going in is worse. The bruises appeared later.

Every second morning, we went back again, for another injection, in the same place. I couldn't imagine how Samantha coped; I couldn't even watch. But, each time the orderly stroked the hair, the nurse was businesslike and Samantha made no sound.

Her stomach swelled. It was discoloured and she looked pregnant. She wanted to go home. Every night, we drank away her sorrows.

Finally, on a Sunday, the course of treatment finished. The hospital was quiet. A few more moments of agony and we would be free. It was over. But then the nurse and orderly indicated we should follow them.

They took us into a back room, where food was laid out. They motioned for us to sit down. "I can't do this," Samantha said. However, manners made us stay, though we turned down the food which was covered in flies. We sipped at some mint tea. The nurse spoke to us in Turkish, as though we were old friends, then the orderly got out a guitar and started to sing for us. It was totally surreal.

Yet even the friendliness could not make everything all right. Even the local doctor offering us a free holiday next year in his apartment block and our favourite waiters boarding the coach as we left to give Samantha flowers couldn't change the memory.

We will not be returning to Turkey.

Independent on Sunday

Task 4

- **Which facts and opinions give an impression of the staff at the hospital, and how do we react to them?**
- **How does the writer structure his text?**
- **How is language used to make the story come to life for the reader?**

- Read the text carefully and answer in detail.
- Explain the effects that are created, and how.
- Quote appropriately to prove the points you make.

Unit 5 Reading Poetry from Different Cultures and Traditions

Targets

To focus on:

1. **the important features of the poems**
2. **appropriate annotation**
3. **how to write about poems.**

In the January before your examination, you receive a pre-release booklet, which includes eight to ten Poems from Different Cultures and Traditions. You will prepare the poems so that you can write about one of them in the examination. However, there will not be a separate question about the poem: you will have to compare it with a previously unseen poem that will be printed on the examination paper.

When analysing poems, concentrate on their significant features:

Content	story, themes, messages
How a different culture is presented	what the poem is saying about life within a culture regarded as different from a traditional British one
Structure	verse form and the ordering of ideas
Rhythm and rhyme	the mood created
Linguistic devices	how language is used, including similes, metaphors, alliteration, onomatopoeia, enjambement, repetition, symbols

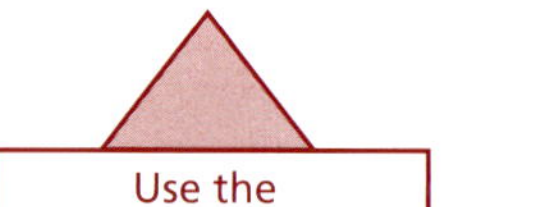

Use these features as a checklist when revising the poems. If you can write about these features, you should have no problems with the questions.

Content

There are several aspects of content:

1. The story: if there is a narrative within the poem, what actually happens?
2. Themes: what general ideas is the poem dealing with: love, hate, family life, the world of work, growing up ... ?
3. The message: what is the poem trying to tell us? That life is miserable, then we die, or love conquers all, or that, inevitably we all grow old, or ... ?

The appropriate annotation of your poems will help you focus on areas such as these and prepare for the examination. However, remember to annotate in pencil, so you can later rub out those jottings you do not really need.

For 2004, annotated texts are allowed in the examination. However, annotations must consist only of single words or very brief phrases, underlining or highlighting. The annotations in the example below would have to be briefer for the exam itself.

After 2004, you can annotate your poems as part of the preparation, but you will be given a new copy of the poems to use with your examination paper. If you wish, you can annotate that in the exam itself, as fully as you wish.

Task 1

Choose a poem from the pre-released booklet and annotate it, showing where significant features of content appear.

For example:

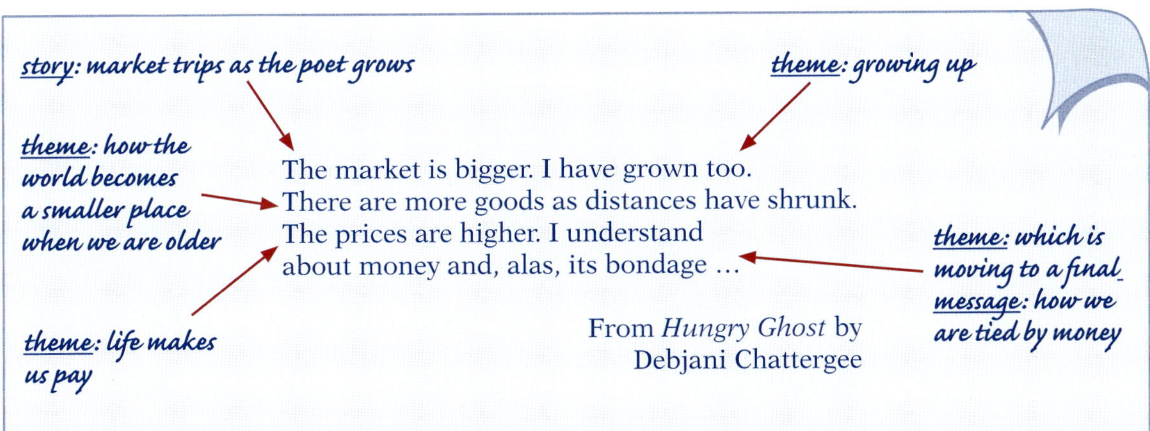

Task 2

Complete the same process with the other poems.

How a different culture is presented

Involved with the content of each poem is its presentation of a different culture. You are required to write about that aspect in the examination and will do it by analysing the particular setting(s) and/or situation(s) presented by the poet, as required by the question.

BWALLA THE HUNTER by Oodgeroo of the tribe Noonuccal

In the hard famine time, in the long drought
Bwalla the hunter on walkabout,
Lubra and children following slow,
All proper hungry long time now

No more kangaroo out on the plain,
Gone to other country where there was rain.
Couldn't find emu, couldn't find seed,
And the children all cry for feed.

They saw great eagle come through the sky
To his big stick gunya in a gum near by,
Fine young wallaby carried in his feet:
He bring tucker for his kids to eat.

Big fella eagle circled slow,
Little fella eagles fed below.
"Gwa!" said Bwalla the hunter, "he
Best fella hunter, better than me."

He dropped his boomerang. "Now I climb,
All share tucker in the hungry time.
We got younks too, we got need-
You make fire and we all have feed."

Then up went Bwalla like a native cat,
All the blackfellows climb like that.
And when he looked over big nest rim
Those young ones all sing out at him.

They flapped and spat, they snapped and clawed,
They plenty wild with him, my word,
They shrilled at tucker-thief big and brown,
But Bwalla took the wallaby and then climbed down.

Question: What impression of Bwalla's life do we get in the first stanza?

Here are two extracts from candidates:

F Grade
Bwalla is a hunter. He walks around and his children are all proper hungry long time now.

A* Grade
Bwalla lives in Australia, since he goes 'on walkabout', but his life is hard. We guess from his name that he is an Aborigine who has to cope with famine and drought. As he is a hunter, with no fixed home, he and his family are forced to wander the land and it drains them (they are 'following slow'). They cannot find enough food, and we hear the pattern of their speech as they explain they have been:

'All proper hungry long time now.'

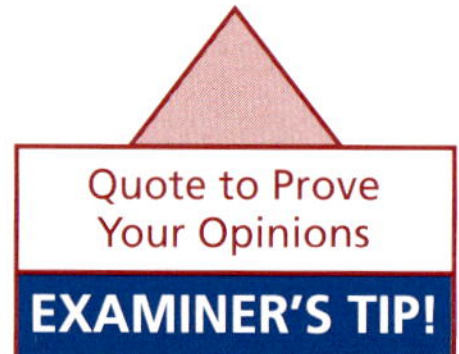

Task 3

What makes the second answer so much better?

Task 4

Clearly identify the culture and situations in each of your pre-released poems, either by:

- **listing the appropriate details**
  or by:
- **annotating the booklet.**

Make your notes brief at this point. You can expand upon them in the examination.

Structure

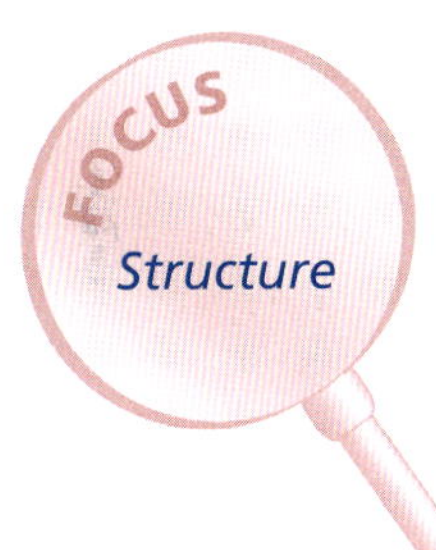

When examining structure, you need to consider:

- verse form: whether there are regular stanzas, or it is free verse; whether there is a chorus or refrain; whether there is a pattern which gives a particular effect
- how the material is organised: whether it is a chronological narrative or a series of connected ideas or otherwise; how the opening and ending relate to each other and the way the body of the poem is developed.

Ask yourself, does the structure:

- organise the ideas clearly or encourage you to sort out the strands; lead you on from point to point or surprise you; begin at the beginning or otherwise; make the message appear simple or complex?
- give an impression of movement, lack of change, a chant or song, a meditation or prayer, clutter or calm?

And, most importantly, you should demonstrate **how** the effect is achieved.

Task 5

How do the structures affect our reactions in these examples?

1. At fourteen I married My Lord you.
I never laughed, being bashful …

At fifteen I stopped scowling,
I desired my dust to be mingled with yours …

At sixteen you departed …

From 'The River-merchant's Wife: A Letter'
by Rihaku, trans. by Ezra Pound

2. You, who went out of Cuba,
tell me,
where will you find green after green,
blue after blue,
palm after palm under the sky?
Tell me.

You, who have forgotten your language,
tell me,
and chew in an alien tongue
the *güel* and the *yu*,
how can you live in silence?
Tell me.

From 'Tell Me' by Nicolás Guillén

Rhythm and rhyme

When you read a poem, the **rhythm** gives the verse a mood. For example:

'And limbo stick is the silence in front of me
limbo

limbo
limbo like me
limbo
limbo like me'

– gives a sense of the dance and the rhythm of the dancer.

'The skin cracks like a pod.
There is never enough water.'

– short, simple sentences make this seem straightforward, everyday, barren and painful.

Rhyme can have a variety of effects. For example:

1. Working with rhythm to give a sense of busyness:

   'You rang your bell and I answered.
   I polished your parquet floor.
   I scraped out your grate
   And I washed your plate
   And I scrubbed till my hands were raw.'

2. Linking ideas – here, the goat and the poet, with 'goat' and 'throat' appropriately 'sharp' because of the final 't' sound:

   'As he moves the knife across the neck of the goat
   I can feel its point on my throat ...'

Task 5

PRACTICE

Locate examples of rhyme and rhythm in two of the pre-released poems and explain their effects.

Linguistic devices

Any study of English is based on language and how it has been used. Examining the poems, you should prepare to analyse:

- similes and metaphors
- alliteration, onomatopoeia and enjambements
- individual words, phrases, lines and sentences.

For good grades, it is not enough to locate the devices. The focus is on:

- what they add to the poem and the reader's understanding
- why they have been used
- how they affect meaning.

Similes and metaphors

Similes and metaphors make comparisons.

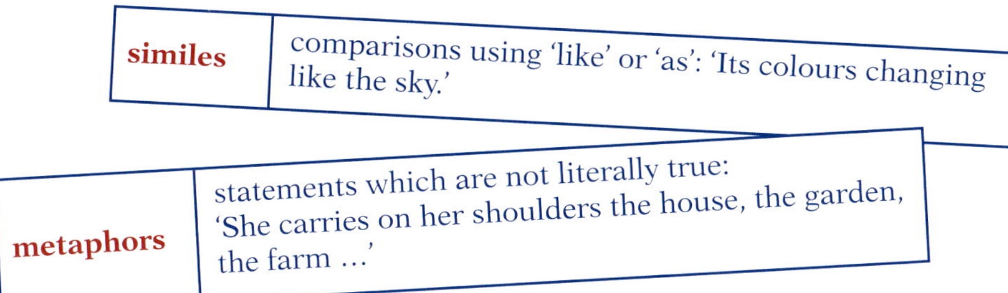

similes	comparisons using 'like' or 'as': 'Its colours changing like the sky.'
metaphors	statements which are not literally true: 'She carries on her shoulders the house, the garden, the farm …'

In the examination, you should explain how the comparison is working. So, for example:

'I want to give up being a bullet
I've been a bullet too long

I want to be an innocent coin
in the hand of a child …'

Here, the poet seems keen to change his life and become more peaceful. The fact that he considers himself to be a bullet makes us feel he is violent and harming someone; but the metaphor in the second stanza takes us back to childhood, a time when the aim was not to hurt others.

'I would float
like a restless spirit, hungry for life.'

With this simile, the poet compares his past with that of a spirit, floating lightly and free and with a passion for what is to come, as if he wants to eat up experiences: 'hungry for life.'

Task 7

Explain the effect of the similes and metaphors within any of the pre-released poems.

Alliteration, onomatopoeia, enjambements, repetition and symbols

Device	Definition	Example	Explanation
alliteration	two or more consecutive words begin with the same letter	'spicy scents'	's' sounds give impression of sizzling excitement
onomatopoeia	the creation of a sound, using words	'Pots and pans bang together in celebration, clang ...'	the verse carries the sounds of the crashing in the kitchen
enjambement	there is no punctuation at the end of a line of poetry, as the sentence runs on to the next line	'Thomas, yuh can tell mi why yuh put de toad Eena Elvira sandwich bag?'	lack of punctuation or completion after 'toad' leaves reader eager to learn where the toad was put
repetition	words or sounds repeated to create an effect	'I desired my dust to be mingled with yours For ever and for ever and for ever.'	enjambement makes the event stretch out, as it does to the next line; repetition stresses it can last to infinity
symbol	something representing something else	'island man wakes up to the sound of blue surf in his head'	the surf represents the life he had in the Caribbean

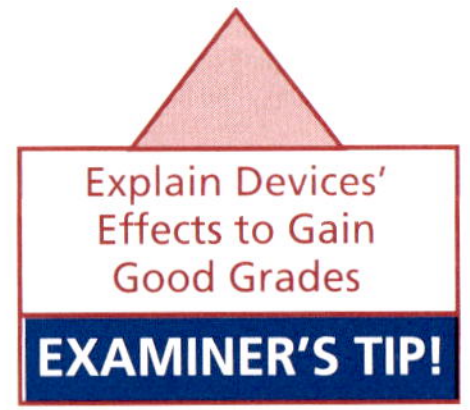

Avoid the temptation to simply 'spot' these devices: to achieve good marks, you must explain their effect.

This is from *Not my Business* by Niyi Osundare:

'And then one evening
As I sat down to eat my yam
A knock on the door froze my hungry hand.
The jeep was waiting on my bewildered lawn
Waiting, waiting in its usual silence.'

An A* student responded to the extract like this:

When the agents of the government arrive, we first have enjambements, which make the evening seem relaxed, as if it is stretching out, but then there is the knock on the door, and that sound – presented to us through onomatopoeia – brings terror. There is the metaphor of fear, as the poet 'froze'. Suddenly, the alliterated phrase 'hungry hand' seems breathless, the 'h's slowing the verse as the metaphor emphasises the fact that he has been hungry, caring only for what he could get for himself, but now his hunger has led him to terror. The fact that 'yam' and 'hand' do not quite rhyme emphasises that his life no longer has balance and harmony.

The enjambement on the penultimate line makes it seem that the experience is beyond time, and might well have no end; the whole world has turned upside down, so that the lawn, a symbol of pleasant normality, is 'bewildered'; and the poem ends with the ominous repetition of 'waiting'. This is an experience from which he will not be able to escape. We can almost hear the engine ticking over in the rhythm of the line:

'Waiting, waiting in its usual silence.'

Task 8

In the student's response, the technical features have been highlighted, to illustrate how many features have been examined.
Analyse a poem of your choice in a similar way.
Remember to:

- **prove your points**
- **explain how the linguistic devices are working.**

- Be aware of all the different elements in the poems.
- Consider how effects are achieved, not just the meaning of the poems.
- Annotate the pre-released material to focus on important details.
- Employ appropriate vocabulary when analysing poetry and prove the points you make.

Unit 6 Reading the Unseen Poem

Targets

To learn:

1. **how to deal with the unseen poem**
2. **how to structure answers**
3. **how to write about poems.**

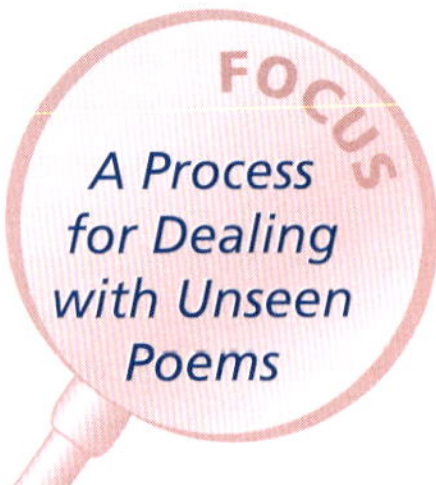

Section A of English Paper 2 requires candidates to compare one of the pre-released poems with an unseen poem, which is printed on the examination paper. There will be one question, though it might be broken into various parts.

To be able to deal with the unseen poem, you need a system for:

- understanding
- interpreting
- analysing the text.

In 5–10 minutes you need to:

1. Read the question and underline its main requirements, so you know what the examiner wants.
2. Read the poem.
3. Work out what is happening, bearing the question in mind.
4. Decide what the poem is suggesting: its themes and message.

Then, depending upon the exact nature of the question:

5. Examine the poem's structure.
6. Identify its most relevant linguistic features.

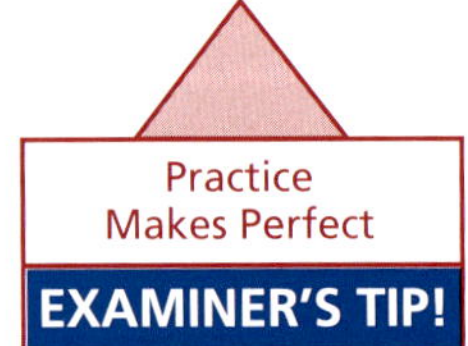

This process has to be completed quickly, because you have only 45 minutes to write about the unseen <u>and</u> the pre-released poem.

The more poems you read, the easier it is to analyse them.

Consider this question:

What impression of farming life in the United States do we get from 'Hay for the Horses' by Gary Snyder?

In your answer, explain:

- **what details of the country are presented to the reader**
- **what we learn about the farm**
- **the work that is involved**
- **the attitude of the farmer.**

Hay for the Horses by Gary Snyder

HE had driven half the night
From far down San Joaquin
Through Mariposa, up the
Dangerous mountain roads,
And pulled in at eight a.m.
With his big truckload of hay
behind the barn.
With winch and ropes and hooks
We stacked the bales up clean
To splintery redwood rafters
High in the dark, flecks of alfalfa
Whirling through shingle-cracks of light,
Itch of haydust in the
sweaty shirt and shoes.
At lunchtime under Black oak
Out in the hot corral,
– The old mare nosing lunchpails,
Grasshoppers crackling in the weeds –
'I'm sixty-eight,' he said,
'I first bucked hay when I was seventeen.
I thought, that day that I started,
I sure would hate to do this all my life.
And dammit, that's just what
I've gone and done.'

Priorities in the answer

1. Throughout, focus on farming in the United States.

2. Logical approach to the question:

   Introduction:
   General statements about farming as presented in the poem; and, perhaps, the fact that it is a different picture from what we might expect in Britain.

   Sections of answer:
   At least four, focusing on the bullets:
   - country
   - farm
   - work
   - farmer.

   Conclusion:
   Final impressions, perhaps offering a personal opinion of the poem.

3. Ensure that points are proved and explained:

Make a point

The reader is presented with a different culture, as we can recognise by both the setting and the language used:
'Out in the hot corral,
– The old mare nosing lunchpails,
Grasshoppers crackling in the weeds ...'
'Corral' immediately presents a picture of a western ranch; 'lunchpails' might be common in America, but not in Britain; and the onomatopoeia – 'Grasshoppers crackling' – brings in a sound that clearly sets the poem in another country.

Quote

Explain

PRACTICE

Task 1

Bearing the question in mind, list the annotations you would add to the poem in an examination.

Make the four sections clear:
- **country**
- **farm**
- **work**
- **farmer.**

This is an introduction to a response to the question:

> Rose-Marie
> 'Hay for the Horses' is about an old man getting hay for his horses. We find out about where he drove and how old he was. He was sixty-eight. He had a barn and there were grasshoppers.

Task 2

1. **How many details have been made relevant here?**
2. **How much of Rose-Marie's introduction needs to be re-written to fit the title?**

Read this alternative:

> Hanif
> In the poem, we are presented with a vivid picture of farming life in America. We find out about the sort of place in which the farmer lives and something about the jobs he has to do. It all seems positive until the final statements by the farmer, though, of course, we are not to know whether he is being serious.

Task 3

Why is this opening better?

Task 4

Using the notes you made earlier, write the middle section of the essay, using quotations to prove your points.

Re-read the question after completing each half page of your response, to make sure you are still answering the question that has been asked. It is easy to lose focus and lose marks!

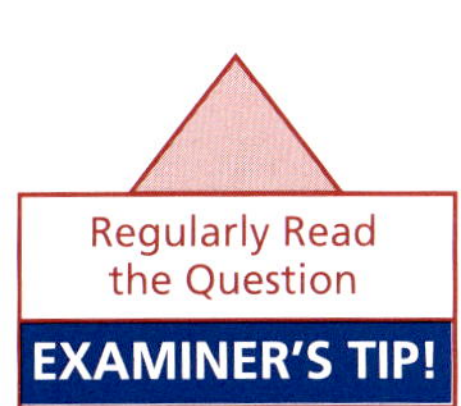

Really effective endings usually link clearly with the opening. In his introduction, Hanif mentioned the final comments by the farmer. His conclusion, therefore, could return to that point and comment on whether the life presented in the poem seems one that might be hated by the man himself.

Write a suitable conclusion.

The Picnic in Jammu

Uncle Ayub swung me round and round
till the horizon became a rail
banked high upon the Himalayas.
The trees signalled me past. I whistled,
shut my eyes through tunnels of the air.
The family laughed, watching me puff
out my muscles, healthily aggressive.

This was late summer, before the snows
come to Kashmir, this was picnic time.

Then, uncoupling me from the sky, he
plunged me into the river, himself
a bough with me dangling at its end.
I went purple as a plum. He reared
back and lowered the branch of his arm
to grandma who swallowed me with a kiss.
Laughter peeled away my goosepimples.

This was late summer, before the snows
come to Kashmir, this was picnic time.

After we'd eaten, he aimed grapes at
my mouth. I flung at him the shells of
pomegranates and ran off. He tracked
me down to the river bank. We battled,
melon-rind and apple-core our arms.
'You two!' grandma cried. 'Stop fighting, you'll
tire yourselves to death!' We didn't listen.

This was late summer, before the snows
come to Kashmir and end children's games.

by Zulfikar Ghose

Task 6

Answer the following question:

What was life like for the poet as a child?
Comment on how he writes about:

- **the setting for the picnic**
- **what happened to him**
- **his family**
- **what is suggested by the refrain.**

Here is some advice that you should bear in mind when dealing with the task:

Question

1. 'How he writes about' directs you, clearly, to examine not just **what** is said, but **how** the language and structure are used.
2. 'Comment' encourages you to deal with the success/effectiveness of the poet in presenting his ideas.

Answer

Follow a simple plan that includes:

1. an introduction dealing with the initial question
2. a section on each of the bullet points
3. a conclusion that includes a final comment or final comments on the poem.

REMEMBER!

- make a point
- quote
- explain

Examiner's Summary

- Respond to the requirements of the title.
- Be prepared to examine the message, structure and language of a poem.
- Tie your answer closely to the poem, using details or quotations to prove your points.

Unit 7 Comparing Poems

To focus on:

1. **what the examination is testing**
2. **how to deal with questions**
3. **practising responses.**

There will be just **one question in Section A of Paper 2**, which you will have to answer. It will involve writing about **two poems**:

- **one** from the pre-released material
- **another** which you will not have seen before, but is printed on the examination paper.

You are expected to take **45 minutes** to answer the question, which is likely to break into several smaller parts, indicated by bullet points.

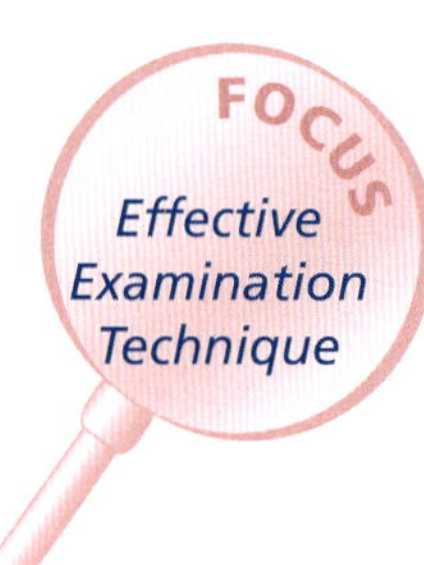

This means that in the exam itself, you will have to:

1. Read the question carefully.
2. Re-read the pre-released poem, bearing in mind the question, and highlight or annotate the poem, picking out the details you will be including in your answer.
3. Carefully read the unseen poem, annotating and underlining the important features as you go.
4. Complete your answer, remembering to be as precise as possible in what you say, using the usual approach:
   - point
   - quotation
   - explanation

     and, when required:
   - comparison.

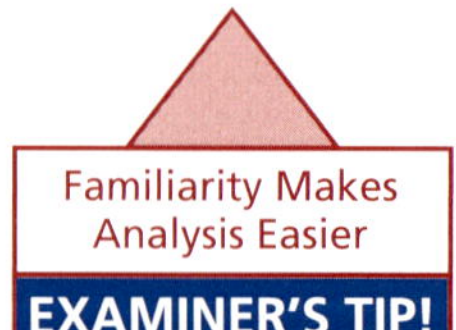

The more familiar you are with poems, the easier it is to write about them in the exam. Time spent on the pre-released materials – and on other poems – is never wasted.

Although questions can vary, the examiners are likely to be expecting you to demonstrate your ability to:

- **understand** the texts, engage with them and **interpret** them
- **select** appropriately from the texts and make **cross-references**
- **understand** and **evaluate** how **language** (and, perhaps, **structure**) is used for effect.

What this means:

understand and interpret	explain the meanings of the poetry: both what is obvious and what is suggested
select	choose the most appropriate details and quotations to respond to a question
cross-references	make clear comparisons between poems
evaluate	decide why certain details have been included and explain, as appropriate, their success

Look at the following example to see what techniques and skills are used in an effective comparison of two poems:

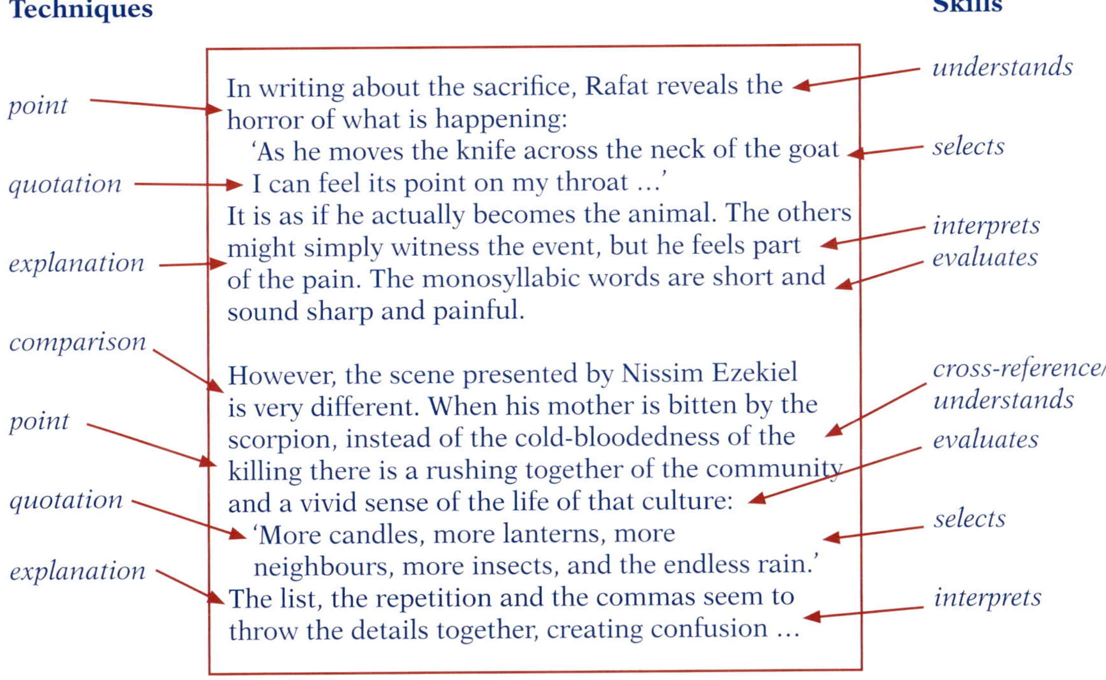

This extract is from a poem set in South Africa. The poet is looking into a restaurant for whites only:

I press my nose
to the clear panes, know,
before I see them, there will be
crushed ice white glass,
linen falls,
the single rose.

Down the road,
working man's cafe sells
bunny chows.
Take it with you, eat
it at a plastic table's top,
wipe your fingers on your jeans,
spit a little on the floor ...

From 'Nothing's Changed' by Tatamkhulu Afrika

Here, we have an image of San Francisco:

At the stoplight waiting for the light
nine a.m. downtown San Francisco
a bright yellow garbage truck
with two garbagemen in red plastic blazers
standing on the back stoop
one on each side hanging on
and looking down into
an elegant open Mercedes
with an elegant couple in it

From 'Two Scavengers in a Truck, Two Beautiful People in a Mercedes'
by Lawrence Ferlinghetti

Task 1

Compare these two extracts, focusing on:

- **what we learn about the people**
- **how language is used to create an impression of the society.**

Task 2

Why have the poems been structured and set out in this way?

This is how one candidate responded to Task 2:

The extract by Tatamkhulu Afrika is in two parts: first there is what the whites have, then what the poor people must put up with. The elegance of life for the whites, with 'white glass', 'linen' and 'the single rose' is contrasted with 'a plastic table's top' and spit on the floor.

The second poem is set out differently and creates a different impression. Instead of the neat stanzas, the lines are of different length and starting in different places. The situation does not seem as settled, and it is as if the poem is moving, just as the people move with their vehicles. It also looks scruffy, as if parts of the lines are just 'hanging on', like the men are hanging on to their garbage truck.

Task 3

What features make this candidate likely to get a top grade?
Look out for:

- **clear comparison**
- **points made, proved and explained**
- **interpretation and evaluation.**

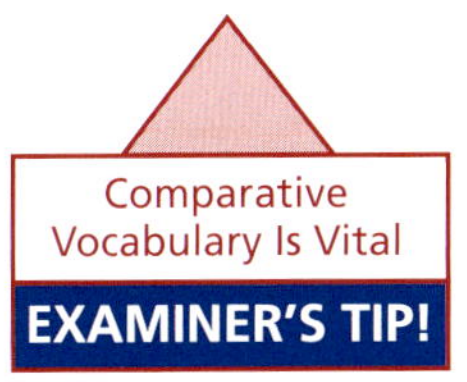

A comparative vocabulary is vital, to make clear comparisons. Use words and phrases like: *whereas*, *on the other hand*, *in contrast*, *similarly*, *in the same way*, *but*, *however* and so on.

Task 4

Having examined the top candidate's response, look back at your own answers to Task 1 and Task 2.

Improve them, making sure comparisons are clear and all the content is properly detailed.

The question in the examination is unlikely to be exclusively comparative. You might, for example, have:

- two bullets asking about one of the poems
- one bullet asking you to compare the poems.

A pre-released poem might only be mentioned in the final comparison. If that happens, most of your marks will clearly be given to the unseen poem, printed on the exam paper itself. It is vital, therefore, that you understand how to approach poems in general (see Units 5 and 6); but then you need to make the final comparison effective, to gain the maximum reward.

Task 5

PRACTICE

Final Practice Question:

1. Read these extracts.

An old woman grabs
hold of your sleeve
and tags along.

She wants a fifty paise coin.
She says she will take you
to the horseshoe shrine.

You've seen it already.
She hobbles along anyway
and tightens her grip on your shirt.

She won't let you go.
You know how old women are.
They stick to you like a burr.

From *An Old Woman* by Arun Kolatkar

While my hair was still cut straight across my forehead
I played about the front gate, pulling flowers.
You came by on bamboo stilts, playing horse,
You walked about my seat, playing with blue plums.
And we went on living in the village of Chokan:
Two small people without dislike or suspicion.

At fourteen I married My Lord you.
I never laughed, being bashful.
Lowering my head, I looked at the wall.
Called to, a thousand times, I never looked back.

From 'The River-merchant's Wife: A Letter' by Li Po
(a.k.a. Rihaku)

2. Answer these questions:

- **How is language used to give an impression of the old woman in Kolatkar's poem?**
- **What is the effect of the short lines, short sentences and short stanzas in 'An Old Woman'?**
- **What differences are there between the lives of the people in these two poems?**

Examiner's Summary

- Identify the precise demands of the question.
- Remember to make a point, quote, explain and compare.
- Use an appropriate comparative vocabulary.

Unit 8 A Writing Process for Section B

1. **To identify purpose and audience.**
2. **To plan by:**
   - **structuring a response**
   - **using a 'language palette' to enrich your writing.**
3. **To write accurately.**
4. **To check properly.**

FACTS
- Time
- Length

Writing skills are tested in Section B of both papers. For Paper 1, you are recommended to take 40 minutes to plan, write and check a response; Paper 2 allows 45 minutes. You will not be expected to write more than one and a half to two sides.

Writing more usually leads to a lack of control; writing less usually means ideas are not sufficiently developed.

These responses produce 30% of your total marks. You will be marked on your organisation and communication skills – your ability to:
- write for a purpose and audience
- produce relevant ideas
- structure and paragraph your writing
- use language effectively

and on the accuracy of your:
- sentences
- punctuation
- spelling.

This unit focuses on the development of **Organisation and Communication**, through a **Writing Process**.

You need a **Writing Process** to:
- give your writing structure
- allow ideas to develop fluently
- give you confidence.

Skill 1: Identification of purpose and audience

It is essential that you write appropriately for purpose and audience.

The purpose	The audience
This is the reason for writing; it is the item you have been asked to produce: *a letter advising a homeless person, an article arguing the dangers of fireworks, an analysis of an event, situation or process,* and so on.	This is the person or people for whom you are writing: *teenagers, old people, the examiner,* and so on.

If no particular audience is specified, assume it is the examiner. In that case, you must still write appropriately. As a general rule, avoid slang and use Standard English.

Skill 2: Planning

You should spend five minutes planning your responses. Without a plan, you are unlikely to write effectively.

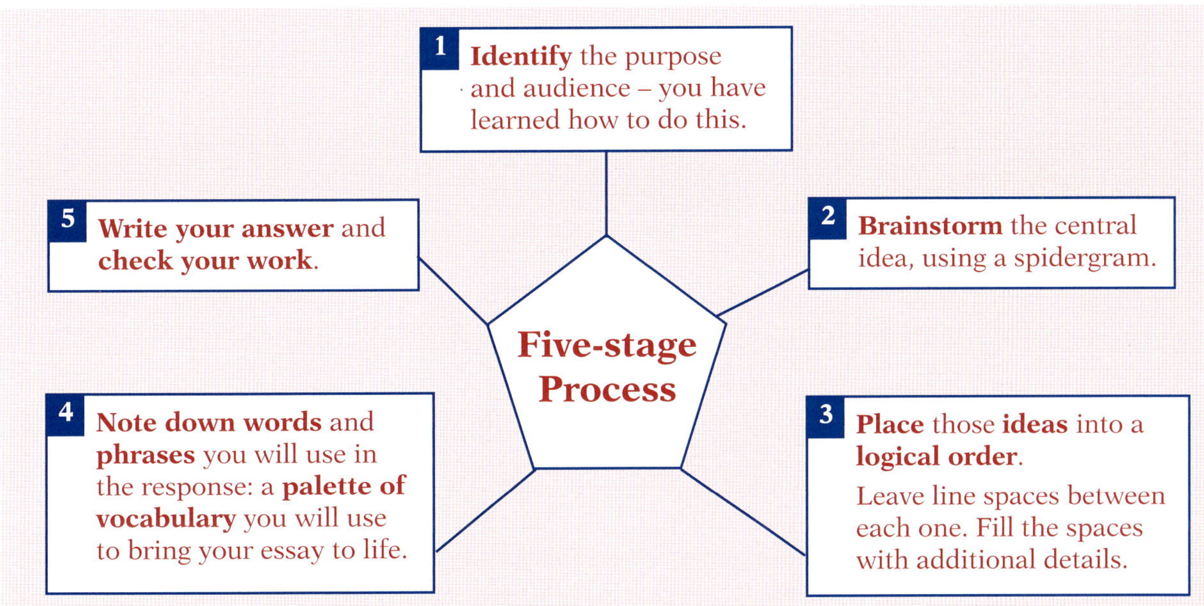

Skill 3: Writing
Follow your plan, otherwise time has been wasted and organisation will be poor. Write carefully. Remember the quality of your work is being assessed.

Skill 4: Checking
Spend five minutes checking your response: correct errors, improve expression and add anything you have missed. Read your response slowly in your head, as if you were reading it out loud. It will help you spot mistakes.

How to follow the process

Skill 1: Identification of purpose and audience

Underline or highlight the purpose and audience in the title. This will help you stay 'on track' as you plan and write.

Read the following exam questions:

Question 1 **The audience**

Write an article for an old people's magazine, persuading the readers to take care in the kitchen.

The purpose

Question 2:
As a local safety officer, produce a leaflet for primary school students, offering advice on safety in the home.

Task 1

Write down the purpose and audience for Question 2.

You will see immediately how the two questions differ, how the emphasis in the responses would have to be different and how different language would be needed.

We do not usually speak to old people in the same way we do to children!

Task 2

1. **Considering the purpose, what points might be included to respond to Question 2, which would not be appropriate for Question 1?**
2. **Concentrating on the audiences, write an opening sentence for each response.**

Skill 2: Planning

When you have identified the purpose and audience, you can use the four-stage planning process:

1. Brainstorm your ideas.
2. Place them into a logical sequence.
3. Add extra notes to each idea.
4. Consider a vocabulary palette, into which you can dip as you write.

Question:
Write a letter to the Prime Minister, to argue that education should be more concerned with the world of work.

Brainstorm

Education

- *preparation for work essential*
- *would motivate lower achievers*
- *basic skills essential*
- *life involves more than work*
- *students should learn about music, art etc.*
- *those with knowledge of working world could support teachers*
- *too much emphasis already on education for employment*
- *too many go to university?*
- *potential to reduce disruption in schools*

Sequence and additional details

Introduction
Work essential to individuals and the country. Must make ed. more relevant.

1. Case for the current system

Educating people for life
Life's more than just work. Where does sport fit? And the arts? Idea of enrichment and ed. for leisure. Learning for learning's sake not a bad thing.

Too much emphasis already on jobs
School students undertake work experience, have careers education etc. Pushed to get part-time jobs. And have 50 working years still to come. Companies already involved in many schools.

2. Why this should be developed

Task 3

Complete the plan. Add extra ideas to the spider diagram if you wish; then develop and complete the structured notes. Include ideas for a conclusion.

Vocabulary Palette

If you collect suitable words and phrases before you begin to write, you can use them to 'paint' into your response, like an artist dips into colours when painting.

Nevertheless

However

On the other hand

Contrary to popular opinion

In addition

The status quo

People make fine speeches, but …

We have to improve our performance

No one dares to tackle the leather-patched teachers …

A totally unsatisfactory situation

Surely no one could disagree

Our children are suffering

Task 4

Produce your own palette. Add several discourse markers that link ideas (such as 'however', 'nevertheless') and one example from each of the following areas:

- **rhetorical** phrases, intended to rouse our emotions ('surely no one could disagree')
- **ironic** phrases that use sarcasm or humour ('people make fine speeches but …')
- **emotive** phrases that appeal to the reader's feelings ('our children are suffering')
- phrases that demonstrate **effective language** ('no one dares to tackle the leather-patched teachers')

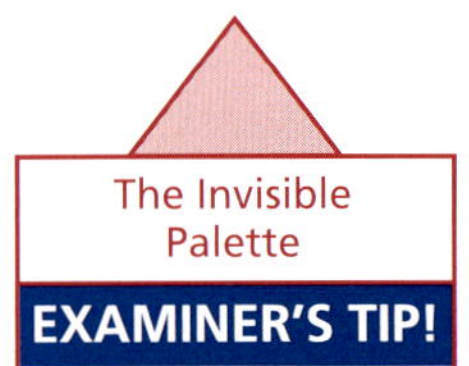

In the exam, you might not draw a palette, but the words and phrases you collect, whether you jot them down or just store them in your mind, will help you to hit the targets in the mark scheme.

Skill 3: Writing

Now you should be ready to write the letter. Of course you will need to set it out properly; but you should find it relatively easy to produce, because most of the hard work has already been done.

However, there are skills to emphasise at this point:

1. **Spelling**
   - Many mistakes can be avoided: look particularly for doubling of letters, use of 'their', 'there', 'they're', and so on.
2. **Expression**
   - Don't repeat yourself.
   - Use words and phrases that are appropriate for the intended audience.
3. **Punctuation**
   - Keep re-reading your response as you write it and correct punctuation.
   - When you pause, consider using a full stop, comma or question mark.
   - If you can use commas, colons and semi-colons properly, show the examiner!
4. **Paragraphing**
   - One-sentence paragraphs or very long rambling ones usually suggest this is likely to be an 'E Grade' candidate.
   - Paragraphs that are all the same length usually indicate 'D Grade' work.
   - A variety of paragraph lengths suggest A*–C standard.
   - Paragraphs that contain flowing sentences and are linked well come from the best candidates.

Task 5

Write the first four or five paragraphs of your letter.

Use your plan and keep re-reading the title.

Task 6

1. **Re-read the advice above and correct your response.**
2. **Count how many improvements you have made!**

- You must remember exactly the purpose and audience for which you are writing.
- Take time to produce a detailed plan: it is essential.
- Write carefully. Don't rush.
- Time spent checking your response will improve your mark.
- The more you practise, the easier the Writing Process becomes.

Unit 9 Revising Writing Skills

Target **To improve presentational, technical and compositional skills.**

Section B of both English papers tests writing skills. You should aim to write:

- fluently
- accurately
- neatly.

This unit highlights the technical skills needed for better grades.

Spelling: what the level means

Achievement level	Requirement
Low	'show accuracy in the spelling of words in common use'
Top	'show accuracy in spelling words from an ambitious vocabulary'

Help yourself improve by focusing on key areas:

1. Ensure you can spell all the words used regularly on your palette, such as the discourse markers.

2. Never misspell words that appear on the examination paper.

Task 1

1. **Ask a friend to dictate to you an extract from a text you have studied.**
2. **Check the spelling for accuracy. Learn any words you have got wrong, using a simple system: read – learn – cover – write – check.**

Consider **borrowing** vocabulary from the texts in Section A. Read your completed response **backwards**, so that you concentrate on each individual word.

Punctuation

Achievement level	Requirement
Low	'write with some control of punctuation'
Top	'use complex punctuation with success'

FOCUS
Punctuation

Punctuation within the sentence is vital for top grades. Good candidates can use commas, colons, semi-colons, apostrophes and speech marks accurately.

Commas

Commas should be used appropriately, and not to replace full stops.

Task 2

1. **Find a newspaper and underline all the commas in three reports.**
2. **Read the sentences out loud, noticing how commas are used to separate lists and add information to main sentences.**
3. **Write three sentences, each including at least three commas.**

Colons and semi-colons

Colons

- follow a general statement, to introduce lists
- or introduce quotations

Semi-colons

- break up complicated lists
- or separate closely related sentences.

Example: *I want to be like my father when I'm older: as intelligent as a chess Grand Master; as sophisticated as a member of the aristocracy; and as gentle as a hungry Rottweiler. Of course, he thinks he's nothing special; all fathers are modest. As he says to us at meal-times: "I am but a humble soul ..."*

Task 3

Write three sentences, like the ones above, which include colons and semi-colons.

Apostrophes

You will have covered these rules before, but a quick reminder:

apostrophes of omission – something has been left out, for example, 'do not' becomes 'don't'; 'I am' becomes 'I'm'.
apostrophes of possession – something is owned, for example, 'the room of the girl' becomes 'the girl's room'; 'the room of the girls' becomes 'the girls' room'.

Speech Marks

All the rules are included in this short passage:

"I can do simple speech marks," said Sadie.
Jamie replied, "I can do them when the speaker comes at the start of the sentence."
"It's more difficult," said Steph, "when the speaker is mentioned in the middle of the sentence being spoken."
"Sometimes it's easier, though," said Sanjay. "Use a full stop if the speaker is mentioned between two complete sentences."
"But put the speech marks around the words that are actually spoken!" said Sarah.
"True! And there can only be one speaker in each paragraph," added the teacher.

Task 4

Write ten lines of conversation, about the current state of your GCSE work, using the same style of conversation as the one above. Include speech marks and at least four apostrophes.

Question marks

You know when and how to use question marks, but it is easy to forget to use them in exams. Don't forget to use them.

Exclamation marks

Use exclamation marks sparingly. You should use them only to indicate:

- suddenness of expression
- surprise
- or to show something is remarkable.

Expression

'C Grade' candidates use words and phrases, which are interesting enough to make the reader want to read more.

Vocabulary

To discover new words, read widely: broadsheet newspapers are an excellent source of new vocabulary.

Task 5

1. Find **five** new words each day in the newspaper.
2. Use a dictionary to discover what they mean.
3. Learn them and put them into practice sentences.

Originality

Avoid clichés (phrases we have heard many times before). Instead, consider using different words, similes and metaphors. Use this approach to turn *'This programme's rubbish'* into *'It's as riveting as assemblies about litter'*.

Try to show rather than tell. For example: *'I was bored'* becomes *'I idly flicked through the magazine and kept checking the ticking clock on the dull cream wall … '*.

Task 6

Using the skills above, comment on the state of British music.

- **Include two similes and two metaphors of your own.**
- **Rather than just telling the reader your feelings, use anecdotes to illustrate your points.**

Sentence construction

Notice how a simple sentence can be developed:

1. I love you.
2. Despite your nose, I love you.
3. Despite your nose, which sports more spots than a Dalmation, I love you.
4. Despite your nose, which sports more spots than a Dalmation, I love you and everything about you.
5. Despite your nose, which sports more spots than a Dalmation, I love you and everything about you, especially your big, fat wallet …

Task 7

Write a simple sentence about food, then build on to it, like in the example above. Start with: 'I love …'.

Paragraphing: what the levels mean

Grade	Statement	Meaning
F–E	'uses paragraphs'	Random paragraphs, possibly very long or very short
C	'employs paragraphs effectively'	Paragraphs are based on topic sentences, vary in length and are linked.
B	'paragraphs enhance meaning'	Long and short paragraphs help to develop ideas, are used to create effects and support the message.

Notice how stories and articles use paragraphs to make points clear, to emphasise detail, to surprise or help persuade.

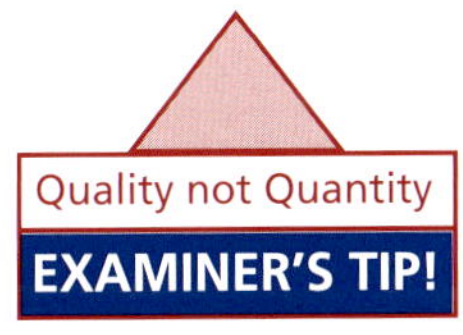

Final Tip

One and a half well-written sides will gain more marks than two and a half careless ones.

- To achieve a good grade, develop and then demonstrate the skills dealt with in this unit.

Unit 10 Writing to Argue, Persuade, Advise

Targets

1. **To focus on and practise the skills needed for Paper 1, Section B.**
2. **To examine the features of writing to argue, persuade and advise.**

FACTS
- Time
- Task

You will have to write an essay for Section B of Paper 1. In 40 minutes you will have to produce a response that argues, persuades or advises – or demonstrate two or three of these styles.

Whatever the question, you should:
- plan for five minutes
- write for thirty minutes
- check for five minutes

following the Writing Process introduced in Unit 8:

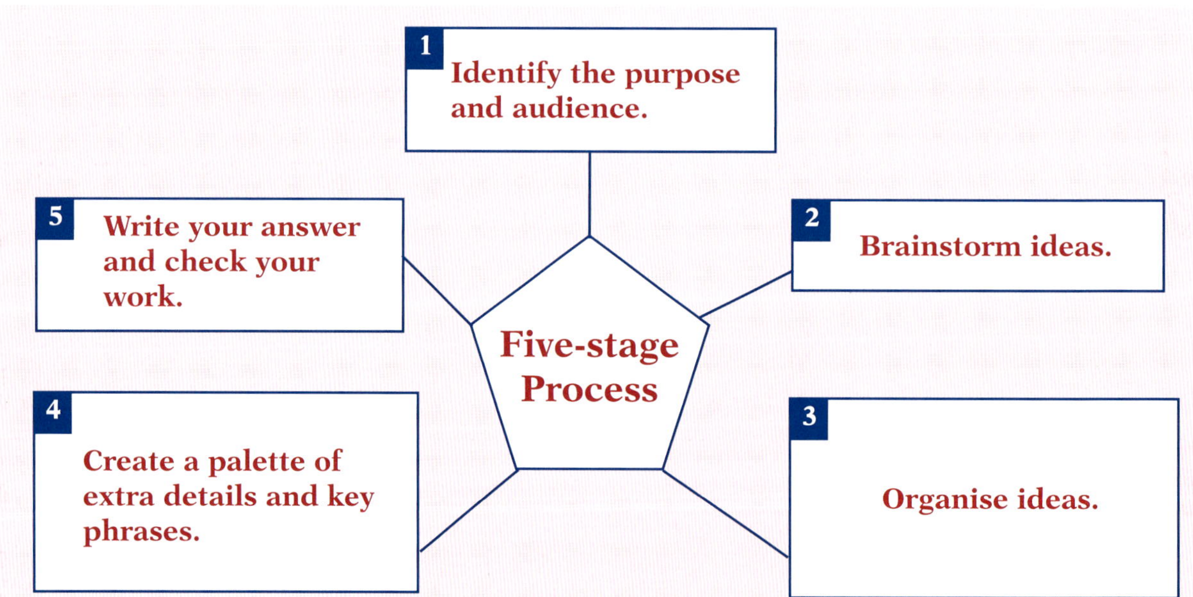

You should also try to employ a range of linguistic techniques.

Rhetoric, emotive language, humour and anecdote

The mark for your response will be higher if you can include the effective use of manipulative language.

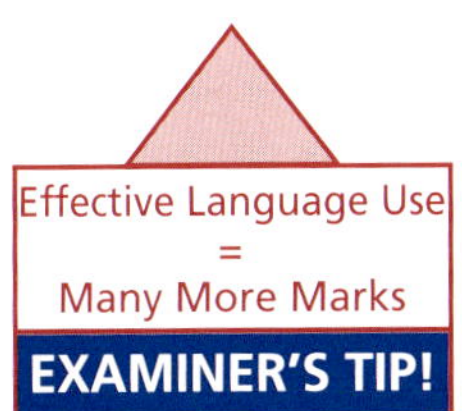

1 **Rhetoric**

Rhetoric is language used for effect and to convince – you can often spot it when politicians are speaking:
Examples: *"This is the time when we must stand together. The challenge has arrived …"*
"Today, tomorrow … until the end of time …"

Often, it is used in the form of rhetorical questions that suggest there can only be one answer:
Example: *Can this be right? Isn't there a better way?*

2 **Emotive language**

Emotive language touches our emotions.
Examples: *Across the land, babies are starving …*
This was a night when old men danced in the streets with tears in their eyes …

Task 1

Write a paragraph, arguing that this is a wonderful time to be alive.
Include rhetoric and emotive language.

3 **Humour**

If you can make the reader smile, you will gain credit. You might use any of the following techniques:
Sarcasm: *After all, nothing is more exciting than the Antiques Roadshow …*
Exaggeration: *He was as brainy as a Pentium Processor …*
Irony: *He had a degree in psychology, but couldn't fasten his shoelaces properly.*

4 **Anecdote**

Your writing will also be more interesting if you use anecdote. An anecdote is a short story, which helps you prove your points.
Example: *I once had a similar experience in the back of my best friend's van. We were driving to Newhaven when …*

Task 2

Write two paragraphs, persuading a friend to lend you some money.
Use humour and an anecdote.

Writing to Argue

To argue, you must be aware of an alternative viewpoint to your own. You should counter alternative points that:

- have been made

or

- could be made.

'Writing to Argue' requires:

- a clear introduction, which is interesting and grabs the reader's attention. For example: *'Sixteen people died in road traffic accidents yesterday ...'* *'Of all the things that are wrong with the world today, one stands out ...'*
- logical progression through the argument, with all sections linked
- an ending that rounds off your argument and convinces the reader.

Openings

You should use the opening paragraph to express what your point of view is and to grab the reader's attention.

Task 3

Write three different opening sentences for the following question:

Question: Write an article for a local newspaper to argue that there should be more activities for old people in the area.

Here are two openings produced by candidates:

Zaheer: Grade C
There is nothing for old people to do round here, and that is really sad.

John: Grade A
Being old need not mean the end of all recreational activities – at least, not if society genuinely cares about those who have given us so much.

Task 4

1. **Why is John's opening better?**
2. **Continue John's opening by completing the first paragraph.**

Essay structures

You can arrange your ideas into a variety of essay structures. For example:

Plan 1	Plan 2	Plan 3	Plan 4
Introduction	Introduction	Introduction	Introduction
One side of argument	One point of view in detail, but with references to other viewpoints	Extreme view Moderate view Your view	Point for one side Alternative view
Other side of argument	Conclusion	Extreme view Moderate view Your view etc.	New point Alternative view etc.
Conclusion		Conclusion	Conclusion

Task 5

Write a speech for a conference about transport, in which you argue that no one should be charged to travel on buses.

Remember to:
- brainstorm
- structure and develop your ideas
- produce a vocabulary palette
- check carefully.

Here are some ideas:

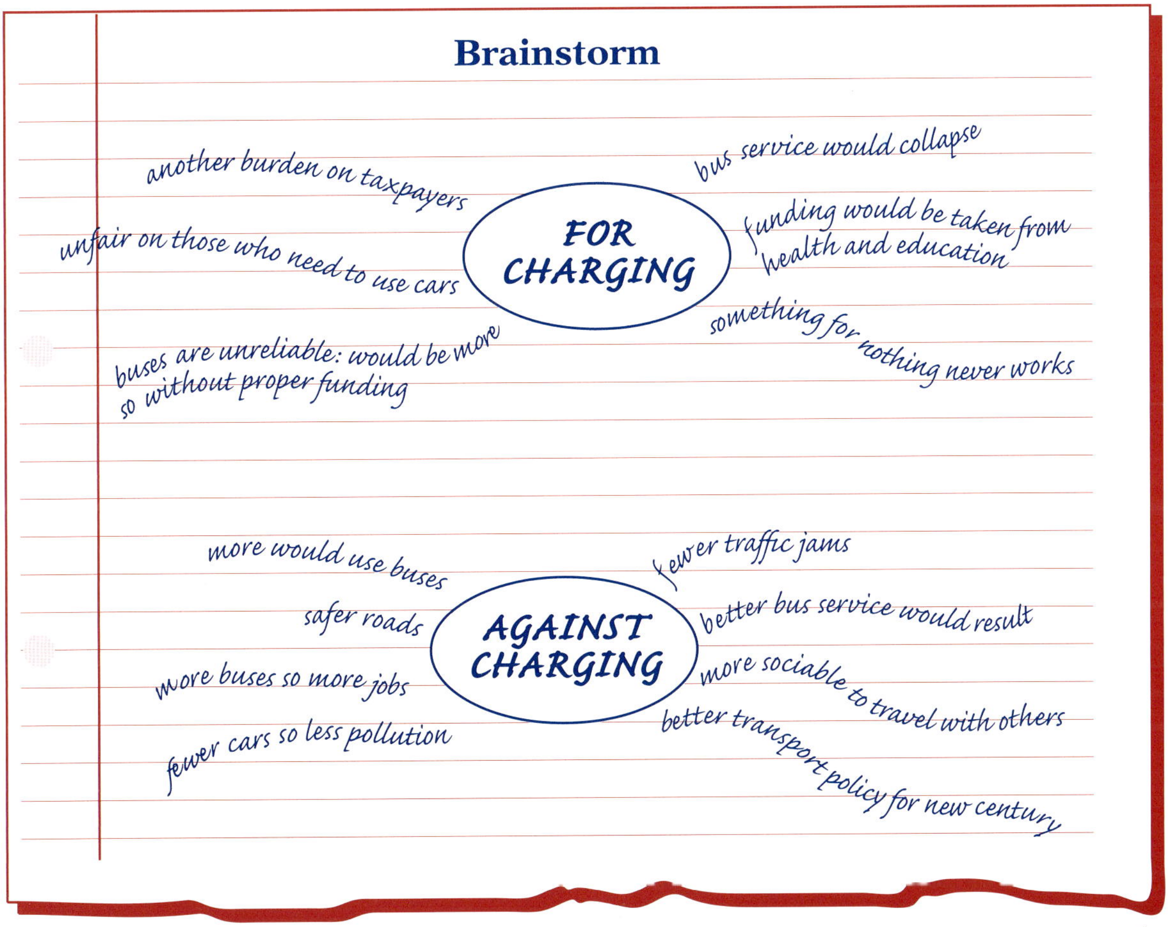

Brainstorm

FOR CHARGING

- another burden on taxpayers
- unfair on those who need to use cars
- buses are unreliable: would be more so without proper funding
- bus service would collapse
- funding would be taken from health and education
- something for nothing never works

AGAINST CHARGING

- more would use buses
- safer roads
- more buses so more jobs
- fewer cars so less pollution
- fewer traffic jams
- better bus service would result
- more sociable to travel with others
- better transport policy for new century

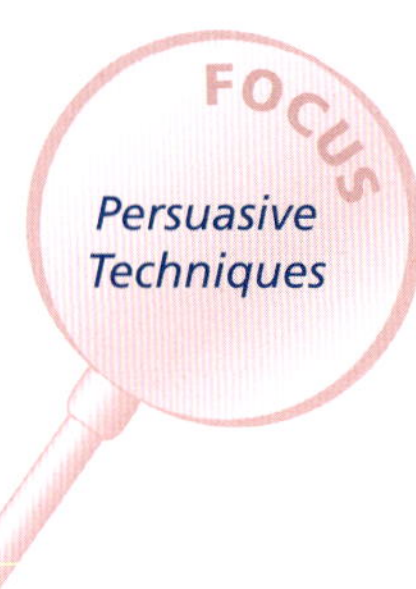

Writing to Persuade

You can persuade by using logical argument, but often when persuading you:

- concentrate on one point of view
- tend to be more subjective, more personal and more one-sided
- try to get a more emotional response from your readers

However, you are likely to employ similar techniques to those used in logical argument such as rhetoric, anecdotes and so on.

'Formal' and 'Less Formal' Questions

In the exam, you can expect persuasive writing questions to fall into two categories: 'formal' and 'less formal'. When answering a **formal** question, you should put forward a case but recognise there could well be a different point of view. Example questions:
'Write a letter to a national newspaper persuading readers to campaign for closer links with Europe.'
'Write a letter to the local council to persuade it that health services in your area need to be improved.'

A **less formal** task is likely to concern a less contentious (or less serious) topic. For example:
'Write a column for a music magazine. Persuade the readers that your relative deserves to be recognised for his or her musical talent.'
'Write a speech for your year group, persuading them to help you raise money for a new youth centre.'

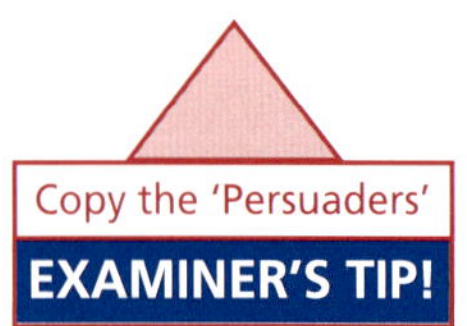

Learn persuasive techniques by noticing how those around you persuade others. For instance, count the number of techniques used by a teacher or lecturer in any lesson; and how parents deal with young children. Notice how teachers and parents use warnings.

Your priority will always be to convince the reader.

Read these paragraphs:

1. When here, you will visit many places like Wales, Devon, the Lake District, Stratford-upon-Avon, Edinburgh, York and London. I'll take you to castles like Caernarvon, Leeds and Warwick. You'll have an opportunity to see other countries without paying a penny.

2. Will you ever again have a chance to see so many places that are highlighted in the guidebooks? You can visit Wales, with its own people and traditions; Devon, full of rolling hills and cream teas; the Lake District, once home of the Romantic Poets; Shakespeare's birthplace in Stratford-upon-Avon; and famous cities such as York, Edinburgh and London. The castles will amaze you: Caernarvon, Leeds, Warwick and many more, equally stunning. You won't have to pay a penny for all this: can you afford to turn down such an offer?

Task 6

1. **Compare the writers' uses of emotive and rhetorical language and visual imagery.**
2. **Which piece of writing is most persuasive, and why?**

Effective endings

The last thing the examiner reads will obviously influence the mark awarded. Endings can sum up what has been said – or add a final touch of compelling persuasion:
'If I haven't yet persuaded you to come and visit us, bear in mind one last point …'

If the ending links with the opening, it can be very effective:

Opening:
'My uncle started drumming on a set of tins when he was six years old and has never looked back …'

Ending:
'Even though he's had chart hits, Uncle Norm hasn't forgotten his roots: when he's cooking, tins of carrots produce a mean rhythm in the kitchen …'

Task 7

Read this opening from an A* candidate and write a suitable final paragraph:

FamAid needs funds to help starving children across the world, but why should you help us? Well, on my last visit to Africa, I held a small child only moments from death. If you had been there, you would have appreciated the needs of the people and the tragedy they are suffering. You would give a donation today, and would give willingly …

Writing to Advise

When writing to advise, you will usually have three priorities:

- to discuss the problem
- to convince the reader you have the solution
- to offer sound advice.

Style and tone

Sometimes you will use a style that is less formal – perhaps when producing some kinds of letters – but you must write appropriately for the audience and for the examiner.

For example:

Response 1	Response 2
Unwise!	***Better***
Eddie! *Oright? How's yer bird? Bin suppin again, have yer? Yer need to get yer life sorted, mate …*	*Dear Eddie,* *Thanks for the letter – though it sounds as if you need some sound advice if you are going to get things sorted out with your girlfriend …*

Task 8

Write another two paragraphs of Response 2, in a similar style.

When advising, you might choose to use:

- an **imperative tone**:
  Make a decision and stick with it … Avoid those pitfalls … Get on with your life!
- more **subtle persuasion**:
  It might be worth considering … I'm sure most people in this situation would …

Structure

As well as using a suitable style, an effective structure, with ideas linked logically, is vital, if the advice is to be accepted. Discourse markers will help you:

- sequence ideas
- demonstrate cause and effect
- be convincing.

For example:

Sequence
Firstly … in addition … then … at the same time

Cause and effect
As a result … The effect of this is likely to be that … This will mean that …

Task 9

Write the ending of your letter to Eddie, ensuring you use imperatives to hammer home your advice.

Top Quality Advice

This extract is from a top candidate, writing as an Agony Aunt in a newspaper and offering advice about relationships:

Above all, consider the future. Right now, it seems easiest to run away and forget all about parents who are trying to stop you enjoying true happiness. However, it is never that simple. Will you be able to cope? And will you be able to live with the guilt of the trauma you have caused?

Think long and hard before reaching for the feather of freedom. It might float beyond your reach and you could crash, painfully.

Task 10

Which of the following high order skills, all taken from the mark scheme, are demonstrated in this extract?

- is convincing and compelling
- engages the reader with detailed, developed and objective analysis
- clearly sustains the purpose
- uses a suitable style, the tone of which is appropriately balanced and sophisticated
- uses linguistic devices like rhetoric
- uses an extensive and appropriate vocabulary.

The extract was part of a response to this letter:

My parents say I have to finish with my boyfriend and his parents hate me. They won't listen to us and we're thinking of running away. Should we do it?
Sonya

Task 11

As the Agony Aunt, write a detailed and lengthy letter back to Sonya, offering advice on what she should do, to supplement the answer in the newspaper.

Writing to Argue, Persuade, Advise

It is quite possible that the Writing question on Paper 1 will require you to blend two, or even three of the styles of writing. If that is the case, you will be able to use the full range of skills and approaches that you have learnt.

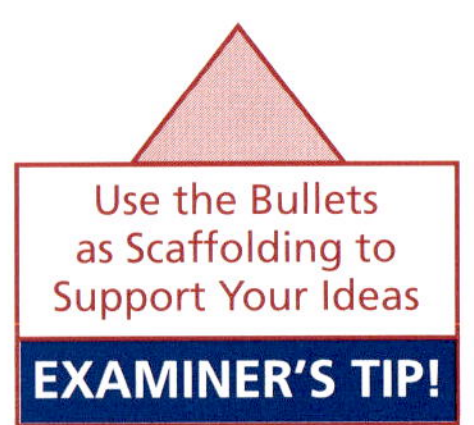

Any question in Section B might involve a stem (or main) requirement, followed by a series of bullet points. You should keep the stem clearly in mind, but respond to each bullet in turn. If you preface them with an introduction, you have effectively been provided with a planning structure.

Consider this example:

Question:

Write an article for a current affairs magazine on the subject of street crime.

- Persuade the readers to take the matter seriously.
- Argue that more needs to be done to control street crime.
- Offer advice to help individuals avoid the effects of street crime.

Possible structure for response:

Paragraph 1: Introduction
Nature and seriousness of street crime

Paragraph 2: Persuasion
Why the subject should be taken seriously

Paragraph 3: Argument
What we can or should do

Paragraph 4: Advice
Range of ideas

Paragraph 5: Conclusion
Effective summary for ending

Task 12

Brainstorm the title and complete the plan.

Of course, you could encounter a question without bullets to help you – especially on the Higher Tier. In that case, you simply need to devise your own structure, though you can often follow a similar method, picking out the different tasks from a single-sentence question. Here is an example:

Question:
Write the text of a speech to be delivered to a students' parliament, in which you persuade students to become involved in schools' and colleges' affairs and advise them on how to organise their efforts.

Task 13

PRACTICE

Examination practice:
In just 40 minutes, respond to the question using the Writing Process:

- plan and structure
- produce a vocabulary palette
- write the speech
- check your response carefully.

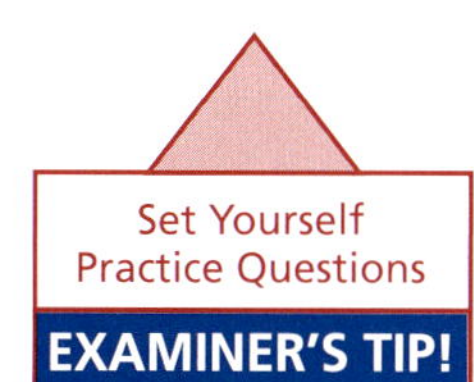

As part of your preparation for the examination, set yourself appropriate titles and respond to them in this way. The more you practise, the easier the process becomes.

Examiner's Summary

- Remember to use the Writing Process.
- Use appropriate language.
- Respond to the particular demands of the title, but always use the significant features associated with each style of writing.
- Pay particular attention to introductions and conclusions.

Unit 11 Writing to Analyse, Review, Comment

Targets

1. **To examine the features of writing to analyse, review, comment.**
2. **To practise the skills involved.**

Section B of Paper 2 will require candidates to respond to a title that involves the 'analyse, review, comment' triplet. There will be just **one task**, which you are recommended to complete in **45 minutes**. It might be related to the subject matter or themes with which you have dealt in Section A.

Analyse means 'examine minutely'

Review means 'look back on' or 'a written evaluation'

Comment means 'a brief expression of opinion'

Whilst writing to argue, persuade and advise, for Paper 1, can require slightly different skills, approaches and styles, the kinds of writing for Paper 2 are very closely related: any analysis is likely to involve review and comment; comment would be unconvincing without some analysis and review, and so on.

However, you will need to focus on certain priorities:

- addressing the purpose and audience
- producing a convincing structure
- ensuring a logical progression of ideas
- giving clear examples to support ideas
- framing the response with a striking opening and effective conclusion.

Priority 1: Purpose and audience

The style of the response will depend upon the **purpose**. You need, therefore, to be able to produce whatever is required – and the key is to read widely so that you can write:

- personally (an analysis of a family crisis, a review of significant events in your own life, comment on what might happen to your career in the future, and so on)
- formally (an analysis of a social problem, a newspaper review of a sporting event, film or television programme, comment on some matter of national debate, and so on).

In preparation, concern yourself only with the style, not the possible content. You will never be asked to write about any matter that demands specialist knowledge. The title will deal with a subject that can be handled by every candidate.

The language you use should be directly related to your potential **audience**. Once again, the greater your general linguistic knowledge, the better your response is likely to be.

These are the openings to two reviews of English GCSE courses, written for next year's students:

Helen – Grade F
I have liked some of the work. But one of my teachers is rubbish. She gives us lots of essays to write and lots of things to read which is rubbish. They are boring. I like the bits where we get to act stuff out and talk a lot. I talk to my mate Gilly who lives next door.

Allan – Grade A
The course offers a variety of texts and tasks and should be suitable for students of all abilities. The teacher has led us through a process of development, so that reading, writing and speaking and listening have been linked as we have moved through coursework and begun to concentrate upon examination requirements.

Task 1

Compare the responses, examining:

- **the topic sentences and the development from them**
- **the language used, including the style and variety**
- **the overall effectiveness of these openings.**

Task 2

Judging by Allan's opening, how do you think the remainder of his response will be structured? What will he include, and in what order?

Priority 2: Structure

An analysis or review is likely to require an overview of a situation and particular details, leading to comment. This can be structured in different ways – for example:

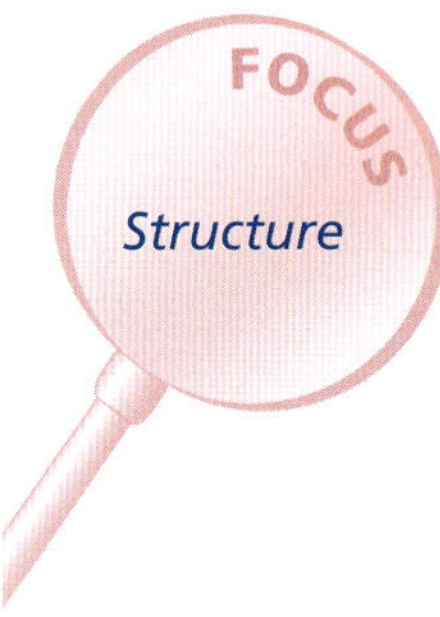

Structure 1	Structure 2
Introduction	Introduction
Detailed analysis/review	Analysis/review Comment
Comment to conclude	Analysis/review Comment
	Conclusion

It is possible that the title will include a stem requirement, supported by bullets, which can provide the scaffolding for your plan. For example:

> Review the quality of life in Britain today.
> In your answer:
> - analyse family life and the effects of our society on it.
> - comment on whether things are getting better or worse.
>
> You might wish to:
> - deal with positive and negative influences you have encountered
>
> and/or
> - mention national trends.

Task 3

Produce a detailed plan for this title.
Remember to:
- **identify priorities**
- **brainstorm ideas**
- **sequence the ideas and develop notes**
- **produce a language palette.**

Priority 3: Progression

There is a range of techniques you can use to make the ideas flow effectively, so that you convince the reader.

1

Rhetorical challenge
There is no reason why your comments cannot be rhetorical, to engage with the reader. For instance:

- *Is it possible to imagine a worse scenario … ?*
- *Can this be as good as it gets … ?*

2

Balanced analysis
You can be more convincing if you appear to have 'all the angles covered'. For example:

- *Some will say that the television is a force for good. However, a close analysis of the storylines in leading soap operas reveals …*
- *You have to admire their resilience, yet …*

3

Discourse markers
These can be used for many purposes, including:
Simple ordering

- *One factor …*
- *Another factor …*
- *The main reason … The most important reason …*

Countering other viewpoints

- *Some people think that … Other people will say …*
- *Despite this … On the other hand …*
- *Overall, though, most would accept that …*

Extending ideas

- *What is more … Furthermore …*
- *In addition …*
- *Above all else …*

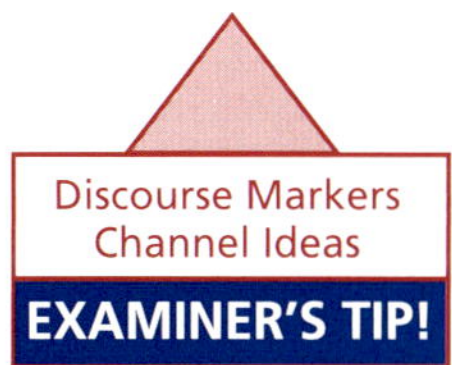

Always make sure you have discourse markers on your palette. They channel your ideas smoothly.

Task 4

Write the first three paragraphs of your response to the question regarding the quality of life in Britain today, making sure you use all the techniques on this page.

Priority 4: Clear exemplification

Without proof, any opinions you present are likely to be questionable. You might, therefore, use:

1

Quotation
Examples:
- *As President Bush said, when he discovered where Iraq is: …*
- *'There is no doubt that this was the most moving moment of my life,' said my grandfather …*

2

Facts
Examples:
- *Only 15% of the population uses a local post office regularly …*
- *J.K. Rowling has sold more books than any other author for three years in a row …*

3

Exemplification: general to particular
Examples:
- *Holidays in Britain are almost inevitably wet. On one occasion, when I was washing my tights in Bridlington …*
- *We should change all the dates of the school holidays. For instance, having six weeks' break in the summer means …*

4

Exemplification: particular to general
Examples:
- *Changes introduced by the government mean that my grandmother has an extra £20 to spend each week. When we consider the impact of these measures on the population as a whole …*
- *The film has three murders, which terrified my children. Who knows the damage being caused to youngsters' minds … ?*

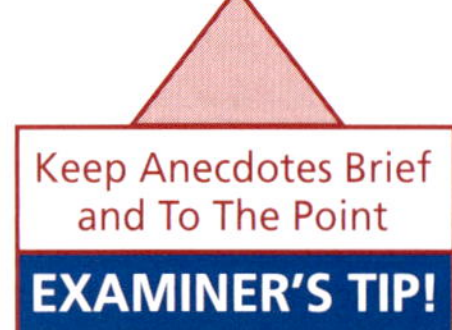

Remember that any anecdotes should be brief – bear the main title in mind at all times and remain focused.

Task 5

Add two paragraphs to your response, including exemplification to make your points more convincing.

Priority 5: Openings and conclusions

As with any form of writing, the opening and ending are particularly important: to grab the reader's attention at the start and to give your views emphasis at the end.

Openings

You can adopt a number of approaches:

1. Explaining how you intend to deal with the title:
There are many attitudes to disability that cause distress to those who suffer, be it from blindness or from a speech impediment. However, the situation could be remedied if we tackled it head on …

2. Using an anecdote to highlight a main point:
Anyone who has seen Molly limping towards the shops cannot fail to be moved, but also they must realise that as a society we should do more to help her. One day last winter, she …

3. Beginning with a relevant quotation:
'I'm telling you, lad, that I'd be better off dead.' How can it be that a society as rich as ours does so little for those with disabilities? What has gone wrong?

When planning your response, consider different openings. Although time is limited in the exam, it is worth a second thought: your first idea is not always the best.

Task 6

Write three different openings to a response to the following title, using:
- **a general introduction**
- **an anecdote**
- **a quotation.**

Title: Comment on the importance of fashion and analyse attitudes to it.

Conclusions

This is a conclusion produced by a student who was asked to comment on the position of women in today's world:

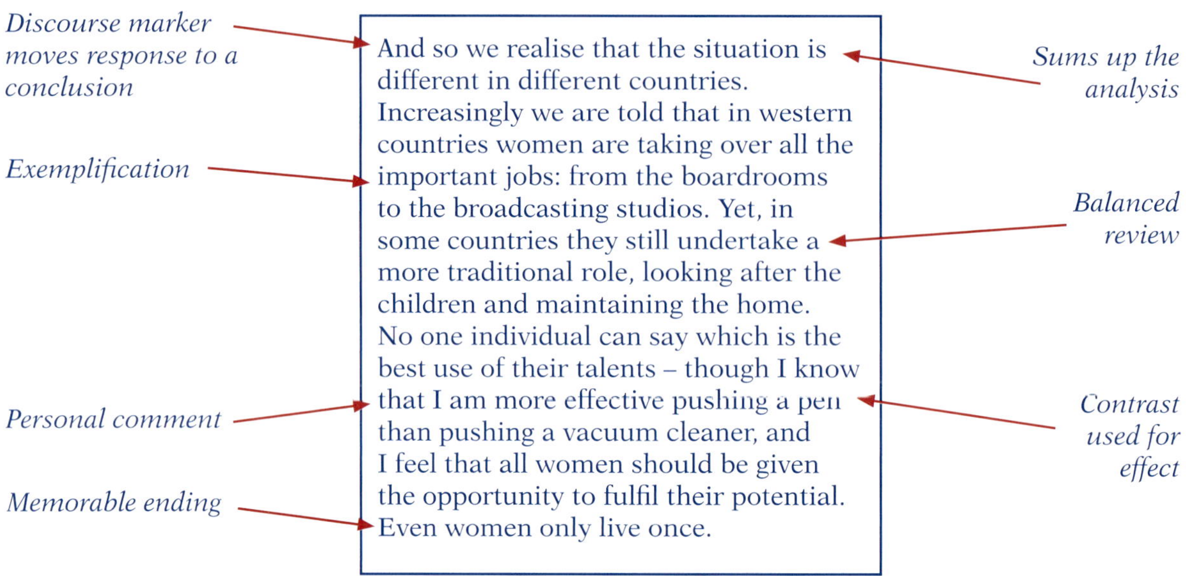

Task 7

Consider these descriptors from the mark scheme. Which grade would the candidate receive?

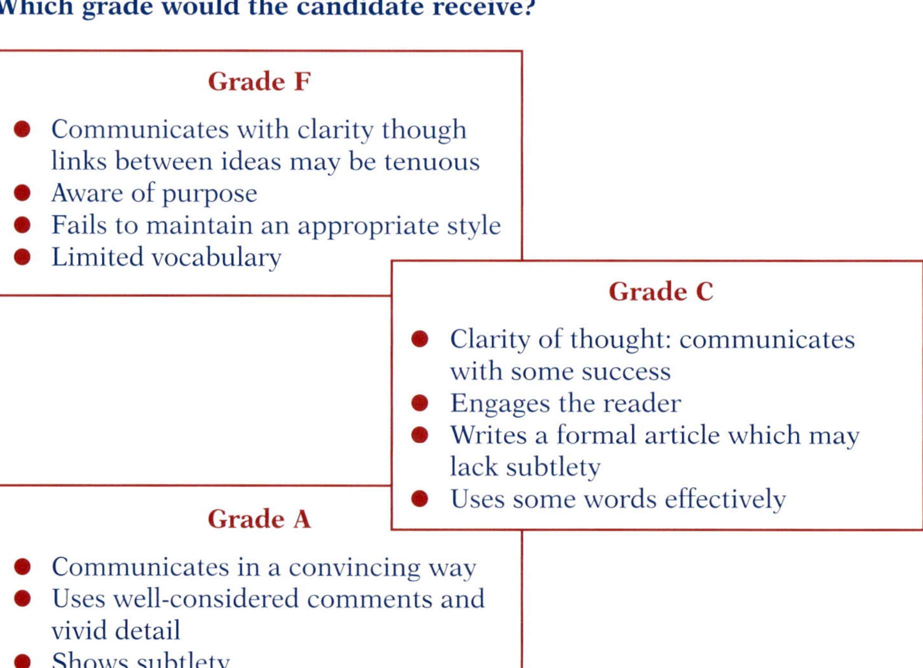

Task 8

Apply these descriptors to the three openings you produced for Task 6.

1. **Which opening is the best, and how good is it?**
2. **If they are below A Grade standard, re-write all three openings, bearing in mind the descriptors and aiming to produce A Grade responses.**

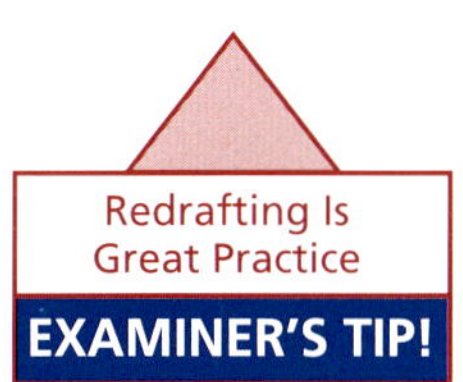

Re-drafting your work is one of the best ways to practise. If you can see how to improve what you have produced, not only will the quality of your responses get better, but you can also use the same skill quickly in the exam.

Task 9

Write a response to the following title:

> 'Everything I have ever achieved, I owe to my parents.'
> Review your own successes, and analyse the significant influences on your life.

Remember to:

- complete the planning and writing process
- write appropriately for the audience – in this case, the examiner
- aim to vary your sentence and paragraph lengths and to vary your vocabulary
- use those features that have been identified in this unit.

Examiner's Summary

- Always follow the Writing Process.
- Structure your ideas effectively.
- Write appropriately for the purpose and audience.
- Develop your ideas logically.
- Pay particular attention to openings and conclusions.

Unit 12 Final Revision for English

Targets

1. To be well prepared for both examination papers.
2. To focus on what is being tested.
3. To understand the skills required for success.

This unit deals with the period leading up to the exam, and 'last-minute' revision.

Dealing with Paper 1, Section A

1 **Ensure you are able to analyse each media text, in terms of:**

- content
- purpose and audience
- argument
- facts and opinions
- structure
- presentational devices
- language.

2 **Revise the technical vocabulary you need to write about the texts.**

Make sure you know:

- the meaning of each technical term (e.g. columns, subjective, rhetorical etc.)
- how to use these words in sentences (e.g. 'rhetoric' is the noun, 'rhetorical' the adjective).

3 **Set yourself questions and answer from your notes.**

- Link the pre-released texts, so you write about them in pairs.
- Find and use individual texts from newspapers or magazines.
- Quote to prove your points.
- Produce responses in 30 minutes.

4 **Think about using the hour for Section A effectively.**

Remember you must:

- read the unseen text carefully
- respond to what is asked
- be guided by the bullet points when they are used
- spend approximately 30 minutes on each question.

Dealing with Paper 2, Section A

1

Regularly re-read the poems you have studied.

- Check you understand each poem and the poetic techniques that have been used.
- Prepare to explain how the language has been used, rather than just spotting similes, metaphors and so on.

2

Try to analyse poems you have not previously prepared.

Since you will have to deal with an 'unseen poem':

- Choose poems from any poetry book and practise reading them quickly.
- Attempt to spot:
  - the story and message
  - poetic techniques, and how they are used.

The ability to deal effectively with an unseen poem will have huge benefits. The time taken for such practices is an investment!

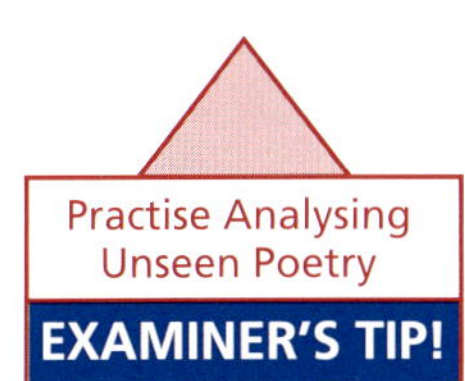

3

Practise

To be best prepared for the examination situation:

- Choose a poem you have not previously studied (even if it is not from a different culture) and compare it with one of the pre-released poems, looking at:
  - message
  - structure
  - linguistic and poetic techniques.
- Produce your answer in 45 minutes.

4

Last-minute preparation

Think about how you are going to respond. Be prepared for:

- questions that range across meanings and how they have been presented in the poems
- bullet points, designed to guide your ideas
- questions that will inevitably focus on the nature of different cultures, by looking at families, settings and so on. Make sure you are ready for that 'angle'.

5 **The actual exam**

Make sure you:

- answer the question(s) set
- quote briefly
- analyse, do not just say what happens.

Dealing with Paper 1 and Paper 2, Section B

1 **Revise approaches to the questions.**

Make sure you know how to:

- use the Writing Process
- write to argue, persuade and advise and analyse, review and comment.

If you have any doubts, re-examine the appropriate units in this book.

2 **Read any available material.**

- See how the writing is structured.
- Notice how the writers use linguistic features.
- Identify where they have used the features which are appropriate for each style of writing, and which you have covered in this book.
- In particular, pay attention to their uses of discourse markers.

3 **Write short extracts to practise for each question.**

For example, produce extracts from:

- an article for a local paper, **arguing** that teenagers receive far too much pocket money
- a letter, to **persuade** your friend to let you have the use of his or her house for a day
- a speech, offering **advice** to school students on how to cope with problem teachers
- an **analysis** of people's satisfaction with local amenities
- an article for a music magazine, **reviewing** the success of a music programme – perhaps *Top of the Pops or The Eurovision Song Contest*
- a section of your autobiography, in which you **comment** on how you coped in certain difficult situations.

4 **Think about how to cope in the examination.**

Remember you will:

- have only 40/45 minutes to produce your responses for Section B
- need to plan, write and check
- have to follow the plan you have set down
- use the time appropriately.

Final Reminders

Paper 1, Section A

1. Answer all parts of the questions that are set.
2. Underline important words on your question paper, if it helps.
3. Read the unseen text quickly and focus on what the question requires.
4. Prove what you say.

Paper 2, Section A

1. Answer the question(s) set.
2. Write about techniques and the message, not just what happens.
3. Don't panic when faced with the unseen poem. Read it slowly several times if that is necessary.
4. Quote, but briefly.

Section B Questions

1. Answer the question set.
2. Always use the Writing Process.
3. Spend:
   - 5 minutes planning
   - 30/35 minutes writing
   - 5 minutes checking.
4. Aim to write about 1½ sides.

Finally

Enter the examination room properly prepared and you will feel in control. The skills in this book can help you to succeed: you have practised them – demonstrate them on the big day.

Examiners want to award good marks – give them the opportunity!

Good luck!

Your Final Checklist

Check through this list to see that you have covered all the necessary skills and revision areas. The right-hand column tells you which unit to go back to, if you need to practise or relearn a skill.

Do you know?	YES	NO	GO TO UNIT
• The date and time of each examination			–
• What each examination involves (e.g. how many papers, how long etc.)			1 & 12
Have you?			
• Learned how to divide up your time in the examination			1 & 12
• Learned how to respond to a range of media texts			2 & 3
• Focused on the importance of purpose and audience			2
• Learned how to deal with non-fiction texts			4
• Concentrated on presentational techniques and structures			2
• Learned to recognise facts and opinions and how they are used			2 & 4
• Learned to analyse language and arguments			2 & 4
• Learned the technical terms you will need for Paper 1, Section A			2
• Practised comparing texts for Paper 1			3
• Learned how to analyse poems			5 & 6
• Learned the technical terms relating to poetry			5
• Practised writing about and comparing poems			6 & 7
Can you?			
Write appropriately for different purposes and audiences			8
Plan an essay quickly and effectively			8
Put together a palette of appropriate words, phrases and discourse markers			8
Display writing skills			9
Write to argue, persuade, advise			10
Write to analyse, review, comment			11
Check and appropriately correct your writing			8
Finally ...			
• Do you know what makes the difference between one grade and another			2 – 12
• Do you know what to do for last-minute revision?			12